college rankings exposed™

Getting Beyond the Rankings Myth to Find Your Perfect College

college rankings exposed™

Getting Beyond the Rankings Myth to Find Your Perfect College

THOMSON ™

PETERSON'S

Australia • Canada • Mexico • Singapore • Spain • United Kingdom • United States

About Thomson Peterson's

Thomson Peterson's (www.petersons.com) is a leading provider of education information and advice, with books and online resources focusing on education search, test preparation, and financial aid. Its Web site offers searchable databases and interactive tools for contacting educational institutions, online practice tests and instruction, and planning tools for securing financial aid. Thomson Peterson's serves 110 million education consumers annually.

For more information, contact Thomson Peterson's, 2000 Lenox Drive, Lawrenceville, NJ 08648; 800-338-3282; or find us on the World Wide Web at: www.petersons.com/about

© 2003 by Paul Boyer
College Rankings Exposed™ is a trademark of Thomson Peterson's, a part of The Thomson Corporation
Thomson Learning™ is a trademark used herein under license.

Editor: Joseph Krasowski; Production Editor: Susan W. Dilts; Manufacturing Manager: Ray Golaszewski; Composition Manager: Linda M. Williams.

ISBN 0-7689-1505-8 (paperback)

Printed in Canada

10 9 8 7 6 5 4 3 2 1   05 04

First Edition

acknowledgments

This book would not have been possible without the involvement of educators from around the country. A special thanks goes out to presidents who agreed to be interviewed, including Dr. Shirley Kenny, president of Stony Brook University; Dr. Arthur Rothkopf, president of Lafayette College; Dr. Bobby Fong, president of Butler University; Dr. Loren Anderson, president of Pacific Lutheran University; and Dr. Alan F. Harre, president of Valparaiso University. They and their institutions represent American higher education at its best.

In addition, insights into the world of college admissions were provided by Marlyn McGrath Lewis, director of undergraduate admissions at Harvard University. A. Tariq Shakoor, director of career services at Emory University, graciously shared his knowledge of the corporate world and what employers want from today's college graduates.

A special thank you goes out to Dr. Jerry Berberet, executive director of the Associated New American Colleges. He was instrumental in guiding me to exemplary colleges around the country.

I am grateful to Laurie Barnett, editor-in-chief of Peterson's, for proposing this project and for providing strong support throughout the writing process. I would especially like to thank my editor, Joe Krasowski, for providing direction and just the right combination of praise and prodding an author needs to get the job done.

The heart of this book—the indicators of quality in an undergraduate education—are directly based on the scholarship of my father, Dr. Ernest L. Boyer, former president of the Carnegie Foundation for the Advancement of Teaching. He devoted much of his long career to promoting a stronger, more flexible, and more integrated approach to undergraduate education. Many of the reforms he championed twenty years ago have become standard practice in American higher education. In many ways, he made this book possible.

contents

Chapter 4

The Five Criteria of a Quality Education

This list provides students and parents with the fundamental questions to ask when looking for a quality college education.

Chapter 5

Measuring a Quality Education

It is not enough just to go to college. Today, colleges and universities examine what all students learn and track their progress after graduation.

Chapter 6

The End of Rankings?

Have we finally reached a new era in how we measure educational quality?

Epilogue

Appendix A

Resources

Appendix B

Questions to Determine Quality

Index

foreword

For the current generation of students, college is fast becoming what high school was for the previous generation—the expected threshold for educational preparation and democratic opportunity. Although college is costly, almost every student who really wants to go to college can find not just an offer of admission, but resources to make college affordable. Obviously, getting a quality education still takes determination and hard work. Some communities remain significantly underrepresented. But at least in terms of accessibility, college is now an option for everyone.

What Matters in College?

Every spring, a flurry of news reports reminds us of the huge numbers of high-achieving students who were denied admission to Harvard, Princeton, Caltech, and Berkeley, or about the odds of gaining admission if you're on the waiting list at Georgetown, Duke, Carleton, or Pomona. A whole industry has grown up around "gaming" the admissions process to win a spot at one of the so-called "nationally ranked" institutions.

The American public loves competition, and so many of us follow these tales from the so-called "race to college." Dramatic though they are, such stories present a wildly misleading picture of the overall college admissions scene. The emphasis on exclusionary admissions processes is a relic of—or perhaps nostalgia for—the days when going to college really was an option for only the fortunate few. Today, of the more than 4,000 colleges and universities, fewer than 200 are dauntingly competitive in their admissions posture. The great majority of campuses are either modestly selective or open to all students who have completed an acceptable precollegiate curriculum. Most applicants not only are admitted to college, but more often than not, find themselves in their first- or second-choice institution.

> *More important, the very concept of "nationally ranked" campuses is flawed at the core.*

More important, the very concept of "nationally ranked" campuses is flawed at the core. *U.S. News & World Report* is the most influential of the college rankings publications, but its ranking system gives disproportionate and distorted weight to college presidents' and other higher education leaders' subjective judgments about colleges and universities other than their own. Presidents themselves say they can know very little about what happens educationally at any campus other than their own. It is like ranking the quality of new cars by collecting the opinions of bystanders who have never driven them.

If college teaches anything, it is the danger of settling for simplistic answers, especially answers that are based on dubious data. So, as higher learning becomes a new basic for our knowledge-intensive society, it is time to steer prospective students toward forms of college planning that require greater analysis. This analysis begins by answering three important questions:

- *In a world characterized by complexity, interdependence, conflict, and change, what kinds of learning will you need as a person, a citizen, and a participant in a rapidly changing economy?*

- *How do the campuses you are considering help students gain these kinds of learning?*

- *What will each of these colleges or universities expect you to accomplish, and how do their expectations fit with your own goals?*

These are basic questions that should stand at the center of all educational planning. But notwithstanding the enormous literature that now supports the college admissions process, prospective students and their families can still find very little useful information to help them answer these most fundamental questions.

It is in this context that *College Rankings Exposed: Getting Beyond the Rankings Myth to Find Your Perfect College* breaks new ground. Author Paul Boyer puts at the center the all-important question, "What Kinds of Learning Matter Most?" To answer this question, he offers myriad examples from pacesetting colleges and universities so readers are better prepared to ask knowledgeable questions about the expectations a college or university holds for its students, and about the programs and teaching practices it has created to help students meet those expectations. *College Rankings Exposed* shifts our focus from the question of whether students will be admitted to the more encompassing issue of how they spend their educational time once they are enrolled.

The New Academy

College Rankings Exposed argues that the interior architecture of the college curriculum is changing much more than the public knows. Students may still be taking the same number of courses each semester and may still be required to assemble the standard 120 credit hours to earn a degree. But both the practices within individual courses and the connections between courses are changing significantly.

Hundreds of colleges and universities now put first-year students in small, inquiry-intensive first-year seminars to help them make the transition from the broad surveys students typically take in high school to the focused, evidence-based reasoning that colleges value. Many faculty members expect students to use sophisticated technology and even online international databases to do their assignments. Growing numbers of faculty also give a priority to collaborative and field-based learning that was unheard of a generation ago.

Campuses of every type now feature new programs and pedagogies intended to create a more engaging, hands-on, and community-linked approach to student learning. The most widely adopted innovations include:

- *Thematically organized general education programs that may extend through all four years*

- *First-year orientation courses and seminars*

- *Field-based service-learning assignments*

- *Supervised internships*

- *Learning communities (two or more courses, connected by a common theme)*

- *Diversity and intercultural studies*

- *Capstone courses or projects for all students*

To better develop students' communication skills, many campuses now emphasize writing across the curriculum. There also are movements afoot to strengthen quantitative literacy and communication skills across the curriculum. Some campuses are asking students to create educational portfolios to present at graduation, both as a way to demonstrate samples of their learning, and also for purposes of assessing the quality of learning. Many campuses are trying to expand the numbers of students studying abroad, while others have programs to involve students with international cultures and language groups right in their own communities.

The scope and pace of these changes vary unevenly, both across different institutions and even across different departments within a single campus. Before applying to a college, prospective students should ask questions to determine what a college or university considers its distinctive educational programs. Additionally, they should find out whether desirable programs such as first-year seminars, learning communities, intercultural studies, internships, and capstone projects are open to all students or reserved just for some.

Students also need to ask how recently the curriculum has been reviewed, what major changes were instituted, and what goals for student accomplishment—both for intellectual skills and breadth of knowledge—the campus has set for all its students. Admissions offices may not immediately be able to answer such questions. But if the public starts to ask them, they will quickly become ready to respond.

New Vision for Learning

In 2002, a national panel commissioned by the Association of American Colleges and Universities (AAC&U) released a major report, *Greater Expectations: A New Vision for Learning as a Nation Goes to College,* documenting the establishment of a "New Academy." This New Academy is characterized by an emphasis on "active learning" (challenging assignments and writing-intensive projects, rather than lectures and tests alone), collaborative and community-based learning, and integrative and interdisciplinary learning.

Campuses with these types of programs still teach traditional disciplines and subjects, of course. But the colleges, universities, and community colleges the AAC&U studied in preparing its report also place new emphasis on world cultures, diversity, ethics and values, and on student responsibility for the way knowledge is used in real-world settings. These forward-thinking institutions also give new priority to interdisciplinary learning and to teaching students how to connect their learning from different sources to identify, frame, and solve complex problems.

College Rankings Exposed takes readers on a tour of these innovative programs and themes. And, by moving beyond the rankings myths and emphasizing how and what students learn on today's campuses, it takes the admissions discussion forward—from its obsession with "getting in" toward a new focus on the quality of college-level learning.

Liberally Educated or Narrowly Trained?

Many students and their families assume that the first educational choice they need to make is whether or not to seek what is commonly called a liberal arts education. Some students will say yes to the liberal arts almost automatically, perhaps because their parents were educated that way, or because a respected teacher or guidance counselor encourages it.

Many other students, however, will automatically rule out the idea of a liberal arts education. Students who are the first in their family to go to college or who are working their way through college, will often reject the idea of a liberal arts education as a luxury, which is out of their reach. They are

Today, the trend on many college and university campuses is to combine the best features of a traditional liberal arts education with the best features of a traditional preprofessional education.

going to college to prepare for a job, they say, and cannot afford to spend time on courses that they perceive as not connected to future employment. With a great deal of pressure from society, many students have come to see college as a form of career training, and the liberal arts seem unrelated to their goals.

But are liberal arts education and career preparation mutually exclusive alternatives? *College Rankings Exposed* argues no. Today, the trend on many college and university campuses is to combine the best features of a traditional liberal arts education with the best features of a traditional preprofessional education.

This new curriculum, emphasizing analytical writing, evidence-based reasoning, research skills, collaborative learning, educational technologies, and field-based learning, prepares students for the requirements of the twenty-first century. Whatever their particular major, students who can see the big picture, analyze and solve problems collaboratively, and make use of new technologies will have a leg up in the changing economy.

Nearly 20 years ago, Paul Boyer's father, Ernest Boyer, former president of the widely respected Carnegie Foundation for the Advancement of Teaching, urged the higher education community to find ways to integrate practical and liberal arts education into what he termed a "new" and distinctively American design for college learning. The trends and practices described in *College Rankings Exposed* are examples of the new educational synthesis that Ernest Boyer worked to inspire.

Given these new developments, students do not need to choose between a liberal arts and a preprofessional curriculum. Rather, the choice is between an education that ensures breadth, focus, intellectual flexibility, and integration across different fields of study and a curriculum that provides only narrow training in a specific area of human endeavor.

The broader approach to college learning is appropriately described as "liberal education." It serves students' long-term interests by cultivating analytical and practical skills; ethical judgment and civic responsibility; a deep understanding of the social, cultural, and physical realms; and the ability to integrate learning across different disciplines.

Some may still believe that targeted training in a specific field is what students need from college. But students and families should look beyond initial job placement. Today's professionals need a richer and more challenging form of education to prepare them for the dynamic complexity that characterizes both the contemporary workplace and global economy. Forms of learning that prepare students to deal with complex questions also prepare them for a world—and a workplace— where change is the only constant.

—Carol Schneider, President,
Association of American Colleges & Universities

introduction

Twenty years ago, *U.S. News & World Report* gave students a new way to pick a college. Its simple strategy was to measure a few key factors—such as a college's reputation, selectivity, and financial resources—then add the numbers and rank every institution accordingly. Those at the top of the list became "America's Best Colleges." With this information in hand, students could "weigh schools against one another and brave the rough seas of college admission," the newsmagazine explained. Now it would no longer be necessary to rely on conventional wisdom, glossy viewbooks, and brief campus tours to find a good school. Students would know—*really know*—that they were applying to the "number one" liberal arts college or the second best university in the nation.

This information proved irresistible. The annual college guide became a bestseller and an indispensable resource for more and more students and their parents. After two decades it reigns as the unofficial kingmaker of American higher education. Reputations literally rise or fall according to its numbers, and no institution is immune from its influence.

When Yale fell from first place to third place a few years ago, university officials predicted a 5 percent drop in applications. Colleges and universities that find themselves in the middle and bottom of the rankings suffer an even worse fate—a perennial public relations battle to rise above their apparent mediocrity and attract enough applicants to fill classroom seats.

> *Reputations literally rise or fall according to its numbers, and no institution is immune from its influence.*

Rankings do more than subjectively try to establish the educational pecking order. Instead, they have fundamentally changed how students, parents—even educators—think about higher education. Mesmerized by numbers, there is less interest in the richness and diversity of American higher education. Instead, all attention is focused on the relative reputation of each institution. What's left is a simple sorting separating the "best" colleges from (by implication) the average and the bad.

What does this mean for students? Rankings send a clear message that it is no longer enough to go to college. What is important is to go to a "good" school—a top-ranked school—where students graduate with the advantages that come with a brand-name diploma. For the most ambitious students, especially, there is tremendous pressure to

> *"I am extremely skeptical that the quality of a university— any more than the quality of a magazine—can be measured statistically."*

get into the handful of schools that vie for the number one slot. The competition to get into Harvard, Yale, and Princeton is so great that these elite institutions now reject between 85 and 90 percent of applications. In fact, Harvard turns away more high school valedictorians than it accepts.

College and university educators struggle to deal with this new force. Most feel compelled to provide the data requested by *U.S. News* and other ranking guides. Top-scoring schools, meanwhile, cannot resist boasting about their success to prospective students and alumni. Yet, behind the scenes, many college administrators are ambivalent about the ranking phenomenon. "I am extremely skeptical that the quality of a university—any more than the quality of a magazine—can be measured statistically," wrote Gerhard Casper, former president of Stanford University, to *U.S. News* a few years ago. "However, even if it can, the producers of the *U.S. News* rankings remain far from discovering the method."

He and others argue that rankings create the false impression that the college experience can be reduced to a single number and that there really is one "best" college. They lead students to believe there is a meaningful difference between a college ranked 28 and another ranked 29. Essentially, they encourage students to scramble up a nonexistent ladder and get as close as possible to a fictional number one institution. They encourage students to look for the right number, not the right fit. "Harvard or bust" is how some college counselors describe a goal that produces unhealthy levels of stress for families and an increasingly unbalanced higher education system.

For all their faults, however, the *U.S News* rankings do respond to a legitimate need. Students and parents do need more information when selecting a college. Unfortunately, colleges have done a poor job of articulating the value of a strong liberal arts education to prospective students. In a highly competitive admissions climate, colleges and universities have become adept at marketing, but the results are superficial and interchangeable promotional brochures and sound-alike campus tours.

Some educators believe colleges are getting what they deserve. *U.S. News* and other publications that rank colleges "fill an obvious gap in public information," acknowledged the editor of *Change,* a leading higher education magazine. Colleges and universities, he argued, must better explain what college is really about. They must develop new and more meaningful ways to measure quality and share this information with students and parents.

College Rankings Exposed: Getting Beyond the Rankings Myth to Find Your Perfect College fills this gap. It provides the information students need to make a genuinely informed college choice. Instead of numbers, it offers a behind-the-scenes understanding of what college is all about and what all students deserve to get out of their college education. Of special importance, it also provides specific questions prospective students should ask when evaluating colleges so that, in the end, they can find a college that is not only "good," but—equally important—the right fit.

What makes a good college? Insights from college presidents and deans interviewed for *College Rankings Exposed* paint a far richer and more exciting portrait of college life than any ranking can accurately measure. A quality college is a place where students work closely with faculty, where they have opportunities to learn both inside and outside the classroom. It's a place where strong liberal arts courses are at the heart of the curriculum. It's a place where students not only earn a credential but also master the skills they really need to succeed in their chosen careers. It's also a place where they gain confidence and are challenged and tested in unexpected ways.

Of special importance, *College Rankings Exposed* argues that this kind of experience can be found across the country and in hundreds of colleges and universities. Higher education is one of our nation's greatest strengths. In this country, there is no one "best" college, but many "good"

> **College Rankings Exposed** *opens doors of opportunity into this wider world of education and helps students pick what is the best college for them.*

colleges offering diverse climates for learning. Students do themselves a tremendous disservice when they reject this menu of options. *College Rankings Exposed* opens doors of opportunity into this wider world of education and helps students pick what is the best college for *them*.

chapter 1
the ranking phenomenon

It's a warm spring morning at a large public university somewhere along the Eastern seaboard. A small group of prospective students, parents, and assorted younger siblings is gathering in the parking lot of the admissions building, looking forward to the first tour of the day. They've already watched an orientation slide show about the university and participated in a brief question-and-answer session with an admissions counselor. It's still early but the level of anxiety is sky high. Nearly every question is a variation of, "Are my SAT scores high enough to get in?" The counselor's reply is vaguely disappointing. "It all depends," he replies.

Meet Robert and Susan, two bright and very cheerful undergraduates who are our guides. Identically dressed in khakis and polo shirts, they are the university's "ambassadors,"

Robert explains, and it is both their honor and responsibility to represent the institution to prospective students. That said, we board the bus and are ready to go.

The large campus sprawls for more than a mile in both width and length. As we drive to our first stop, the guides stand in front, microphone in hand, and take turns narrating the sites. Classroom and administrative buildings slowly roll by as we hear how the strength of the university is its large menu of academic programs and degrees. Students can study abroad, complete internships, change majors, and eventually settle on dual degrees. There are, we are reassured, "many paths to success."

"Any questions?" asks Susan. A few heads shake no.

We park near the library. The door opens and we head out for a short stroll through the heart of the campus, Robert and Susan walking backward so they can maintain eye contact and answer questions. The group passes the oldest and most distinguished buildings and well-groomed flowerbeds and briefly explores the architecture of Old Main where, some-where above, the president's office is located. Classes are end-ing as we are led into a three-story building, move briskly though hallways, and briefly peer into an empty classroom. About thirty chairs are lined in messy rows, facing a wooden lectern and chalkboard.

Outside once more, questions are again invited and this time a mother speaks up. "Are all classes that small?" she asks. Robert hesitates only slightly. There are some large lecture halls, he acknowledges, but adds that small classes are typical.

There are plenty of opportunities for interaction with faculty, he adds.

We board the bus again, heading off campus for a short swing through the surrounding college town. Now we hear about the numerous extracurricular opportunities, including sports, golf courses, a fitness center, and free football tickets. Fraternities and sororities are popular and enrich the community with many valuable service projects, we're told. There are lots of places to eat on campus and prospective students can look forward to "pretty good food." A brief traffic jam stops the bus and Robert and Susan fill the time by teaching us the university cheer. We practice. "Louder!" they encourage. We oblige.

The final destination is a tour of one of the large multi-story residence hall complexes. A special key opens an outside door and we squeeze into a model room maintained just for visitors. Bunk beds, stereo equipment, milk crate bookshelves, and randomly placed posters provide an air of teenage informality. At the same time, the room is meant to reassure parents. No dirty laundry litters the floor and no beer can pyramids decorate the windowsill.

The tour is over. We ride back to the admissions building, say goodbye to the guides and head for home or, possibly, to another school. Robert and Susan are left standing by the bus, quietly debriefing each other on the success of the tour, and reviewing the answers they provided to the two or three questions that were actually asked. Soon there will be another slide show, another bus ride, and another group of students and parents looking out of windows, peering into classrooms, and wondering: "Is this the right place? Will I be happy here? Will my daughter be successful here? Will I have to learn another cheer?"

Three Under a Tree

Welcome to college. More precisely, welcome to college as it is presented to prospective students on college and university tours across the country. At small institutions, the tour might be less orchestrated and slightly less practiced. But it's never done on the fly or entirely unrehearsed. After all, it's a time for an institution to put its best foot forward and show that it does provide all the things that students (and parents) want from higher education.

There is nothing wrong with earnest self-promotion. And what colleges and universities say about themselves is, on the whole, truthful and often sincere. Yet many parents cannot help but notice that after a while, most colleges and universities start to look alike. The students

Many parents cannot help but notice that after a while, most colleges and universities start to look alike.

are different, but the pictures are much the same. In the brochures, viewbooks, and on Web sites, it's always springtime on campus, as students stroll along, take hikes up mountains, or discuss the *Iliad* outside in small groups. "Three under a tree," is how one university president characterizes the typical promotional photo.

And there is always the same language of innovation and excellence. Large and small, east and west, highly selective and minimally selective—the same vocabulary of recruitment is repeated over and over. At this school, students are told, they will find distinguished faculty who love to teach, a wide

> *Even as colleges and universities continually offer more material for prospective students, it seems harder than ever to assess colleges and to know their strengths, weaknesses, and peculiarities.*

selection of interesting majors, friendly students, and abundant opportunities for sports and recreation. Buzzwords abound. What college or university dares to admit that it fails to provide service learning, an integrated curriculum, off-campus study, or undergraduate research? Which will even hint that it provides anything less than the very best preparation for careers or that its reputation is anything less than stellar? What university would say that undergraduates are anything less than its top priority?

Again, educators may believe what they say about their own institutions. But the self-promotion produces understandable cynicism among students and parents. They are the objects of marketing, and they know it. But any attempt to get beyond these generic images and ever-present declarations of quality proves stubbornly difficult. Even as colleges and universities continually offer more material for prospective students—especially online, but even on billboards and radio and in magazines—it seems harder than ever to assess colleges and to know their strengths, weaknesses, and peculiarities. By the time they see the third set of backward walking tour guides, students and parents can be forgiven for secretly wanting them to trip, say something outrageous, or both.

Higher Education Nation

So how did we get here?

Students heading off to college participate in a cherished ritual. Indeed, for many Americans young and old, "college"—even in this cyber age—conjures up images of old world architecture, professors in tweed jackets, tattered books, caps and gowns, and pomp and circumstance. Those who enter its hallowed halls are following the paths of great men and women. Like them, students will be asked to study hard and think deep thoughts so that after four years they can emerge like butterflies from a cocoon—adults ready to become leaders in their chosen professions.

It's fine to respect tradition and to be inspired by the noble heritage of higher learning. But it's also true that higher learning has changed—*radically*. Both as communities and as an idea, colleges and universities bear little resemblance to the fantasy world inhabited by Oxford Dons or Absent-Minded Professors. Neither do they have much in common with the kind of institutions they really were even a generation or two ago. The buildings still stand, the ivy still grows, and the books still fill library shelves, but more than ever before these symbols have become stage props. They represent the

More than 60 percent of Americans now enter a college or university and surveys of Americans show that the vast majority—whether college bound or not—agree that higher education is good and desirable.

spirit and look great on tours, but behind the façade exists a very different world.

What exactly has changed? For one, education is no longer for the lucky few. If parents of today's students went to college, they were probably the first in their families to do so. If *their* parents went to college, they were a distinct minority. Dating back to the genesis of our nation, college was an option—and choice—for just a very small percentage of the population. Congregationalist ministers and lawyers often held college degrees. Some (but not all) presidents did, too. The rest? No way! For us, however, college is the norm. More than 60 percent of Americans now enter a college or university and surveys of Americans show that the vast majority—whether college bound or not—agree that higher education is good and desirable.

America has become the higher education nation. It's not just for the rich or the brightest. It's no longer even just for the middle class and slightly above average. It's for everyone. We're starting to take this fact for granted, but it's worth re-

> *America has become the higher education nation.*

membering. Anyone who wants to go to college will be admitted somewhere. As for those who rejected college when they were 18, endless opportunities exist for week-end, part-time, or online study at any age. Lifelong learning, once a slogan, has become a reality.

This shift from an elite to mass system of higher educa-tion has done far more than change the number of students applying to colleges and universities every fall. It has also changed the structure and purpose of higher education. The old collegiate system was highly structured and, for much of the nation's history, focused on a classical curriculum. If you went to Harvard before the Civil War, your choices for study were very limited. Then, students were not necessarily being trained for a particular job, but were being trained to be schol-ars and gentlemen (it was not until 1963 that Radcliffe women received degrees from Harvard).

Nevertheless, even a cursory review of history shows that this idealized image of collegiate life was rarely reflected in reality. Then, like today, sober-minded intellectuals were the exception, not the rule. Students drank heavily, broke the rules, did as little as possible to get by, and drove their teach-ers crazy. Legend has it that one poor nineteenth-century professor was forced to chase a student across campus in pursuit of a stolen turkey. Still, even if image failed to match reality, there was agreement about what higher education was theoretically about—character development, moral development, and social grooming in preparation for a life of influence and leadership.

As times changed and more Americans completed high school and entered college, the system began to shift to embrace the masses. Over the course of the last century and, especially, over the last few decades, doors have been opened to women, minorities, adults, and retirees. The path has led away from exclusion to a new ethic of inclusion. A new message was being sent out to Americans: "College is the right choice for all. Whatever you want, we have it."

Reaching out to this broader community, colleges began to justify their value in new, far more practical ways. Those who would not have attended college a generation earlier were lured by the promise of job training and career advancement. Here they would learn useful skills and leave with a credential that opened doors to well-paying jobs. New degrees were offered in professional careers, business, and vocational trades, often pushing more traditional disciplines, such as language, history, philosophy, and the arts, to the margins of the curriculum. Studies showed the economic advantage enjoyed by college graduates empowered with job-ready skills and a degree.

Looking for the "Best"

Even as colleges and universities were shifting to a system of
mass education, neither educators nor students were ready to
give up the fantasy of the old elite system. Yes, students and
parents wanted colleges
to be more accessible,
more convenient, more
practical, and offer
more educational
choices, but everyone

*A degree is about getting
ahead of the crowd. It says,
"I'm on the move. Catch me if
you can."*

still liked the idea of college as it was once imagined to be: a
place where a few carefully chosen smart kids sit at the feet of
wise and kind teachers; a place that is warm and nurturing; a
place that promotes both social and intellectual development;
a place with varsity letters and homecoming traditions. In short,
a place that looks and acts like, well, a *college*.

Indeed, as mass education took hold, these symbols of prestige grew ever-more important for some students. After all,
college is about getting something special—knowledge and
skills, of course, but something else—status. Most students
intuitively know that college is about more than learning the
history of the Peloponnesian War or even "useful" things like
how to write a business plan. A degree is about getting ahead
of the crowd. It says, "I'm on the move. Catch me if you can."
But what happens when just about everyone seems to be going to college? What if the statement, "My daughter is enrolling in college this fall" only elicits the response, "Mine, too."
What happens when nearly every resume coming into a hu-

man resources office has a B.A. or B.S. degree listed at the top? College doesn't seem quite so special anymore. "College" isn't enough.

Suddenly it is very important not just to enroll in college but to enroll in a good school, a brand-name school and, ideally, one of the acknowledged "best" schools. These schools have become the refuge for those who are looking for the kind of advantage that a college degree alone no longer provides. You already know the kind of colleges I'm talking about—the Ivy League schools, some of the most highly selective private liberal arts colleges and, possibly, some of the "public Ivies."

The Chivas Regal Impact

This transformation in higher education has created a complex marketing dilemma for colleges and universities. On one hand, colleges must prove their value to the growing percentage of students who are only going to college because it is a helpful—and probably necessary—path to a good job and more money. For these students, colleges portray themselves as flexible, practical, and in touch with the real world. Prospective students hear about possibilities for internships, cooperative education programs, dual majors, and the many paths to success. They see pictures of famous and successful alumni, and hear stories about how graduates get good jobs and go to good graduate schools.

Talking about the practical value of education is absolutely essential in any recruitment effort because it's what students want to hear. "Thirty years ago . . . about 70 percent of people going to college said what they were looking for was a meaningful philosophy of life," says Alan F. Harre, Ph.D., president of Valparaiso University in Indiana. In the early 1990s that had reversed and more than 70 percent were interested in going to college to gain material wealth. "For better or worse," Harre says, "we are attempting to recruit a student body whose values have been heavily influenced by a very materialistic society where everything is dependent upon how much one makes and one's social standing."

Many educators feel this focus on vocationalism sells colleges short. But they have no choice. Colleges cannot recruit effectively if they do not talk to the side of the student's mind that says I'm in college because I want to get a good job.

At the same time, practicality is not enough. Colleges and universities—those that are at least minimally selective—must compete in what has become a high stakes admissions game. Students who do not choose *their* college will go somewhere else, presumably to a college that is more prestigious or, at least, a better value. At no point, and not for any reason, can these colleges concede any ground to their competitors. So in an environment that awards extra points to prestigious schools, all colleges will focus on those things that reassure students that they are, indeed, "good" schools. Using elite colleges as their frame of reference, this means talking about the good teaching and personal attention—but most of all selectivity and top-notch reputation.

This strategy is no secret. Colleges know what students want. "Some call it the 'Chivas Regal impact,'" says Harre, "because everybody wants to drink the very best scotch and drive the very best car. And it goes back to why people are going to school. If they're going to school primarily out of vocationalism and want to be sure they're going to be able to improve upon their parents' social and economic status then they are going to do everything they can to increase their value in the marketplace. There is a perception out there that if you pick the 'wrong' college you're going to end up wasting time and wasting money," he says. What is a "wrong" college? It's an institution that "does not have the level of prestige it needs to have monetary value in the marketplace." In other words, its reputation is not up to snuff and it can't impress future employers. The overriding fear is that "If I pick the wrong place—if Valparaiso's reputation is not as good as they tell me it is—does that mean if I want to go to San Diego and work that nobody is going to hire me because they have never heard of Valparaiso University?"

The result is a nationwide recruitment effort in higher education that forces most colleges to act like they are all excellent in the very narrow way that excellence is defined—primarily though selectivity and reputation.

You Rejected My Son—See You in Court

The pressure of elitism creates its own problems for prospective students and their families. The first symptom is stress. Every fall, stories appear in newspapers around the country about the burdens placed on ambitious high school students who work around the clock to impress college admissions counselors with top grades and a rich extracurricular life. We read about high school juniors who study late into the night, volunteer at social service agencies, lead school clubs, play sports, and consider anything less than an "A" to be the end of world.

At the same time we hear about parents who have gone off the deep end. Indeed, seeing how some ambitious and demanding parents push their children to succeed both academically and extracurricularly, it's tempting to place the blame for all the stress students (and admissions counselors) feel on meddling parents. Apparently forgetting that it is their child, not themselves, applying to college, some parents all but hijack the process.

"Parents write their kids' essays and even attempt to attend their interviews," says Marilee Jones, dean of admissions at the Massachusetts Institute of Technology (MIT). "They make excuses for their child's bad grades and threaten to sue high school personnel who reveal any information perceived to be potentially harmful to their child's chances of admission. As dean of admissions, I see this type of behavior at least twice a week."

And when things go wrong and a rejection letter arrives, it's not clear who is more upset. Jones recalls a letter she received from one father, just three sentences long: "You rejected my son. He's devastated. See you in court." Yet the very next day another letter arrived, this time from the son: "Thank you for not admitting me to MIT. This is the best day of my life." In this case, the rejection provided a happy ending for both the student and MIT (no word on the father's prognosis).

But these stories do not reflect the norm. For every parent who schedules his or her child's life with a stopwatch, there are many other parents who take just the opposite approach. Pamela Lewis, president of Queens University in North Carolina, found that while some students do believe their parents are overly involved, an equal number want *more* involvement and guidance.

In the end, stories of stress and micromanagement may not indicate confidence among students and parents in the college admissions game, but instead the opposite—tremendous insecurity and uncertainty. They're led to believe that a great deal is at stake, but they don't know how to proceed. Newspaper columnist Richard Reeve spoke for many parents trying to help guide their teenagers through the maze of modern college admissions. "It's not that the college entrance and acceptance process has become so competitive and cumbersome that parents are lucky to retain their sanity," he wrote. "It is that the process has become so irrational and unpredictable that mothers and fathers can no longer confidently discharge the parental duty of pointing and guiding a child in the right direction."

Looking for a Better Way

In the college admissions world, where the decision-making process is fraught with anxiety and a lack of reliable information, it didn't take long for entrepreneurs to come in with an assortment of solutions. First came a few gossipy "insider" guides to colleges in the early 1980s, most providing brief descriptions of the nation's most selective institutions. *The Fisk Guide to Colleges* was an early participant in this new kind of guide. It not only described colleges in a breezy style but also awarded stars to schools according to their strength in a variety of areas, ranging from social life to academic rigor.

All this provided an amusing new resource for students, but what really transformed the college choice process was quietly introduced in 1983 by *U.S. News & World Report*, a conservative newsweekly that always ran a distant third to its slicker and hipper rivals, *Time* and *Newsweek*. Beginning that year in an informal way, but with more sophistication a few years later, the magazine unveiled a comprehensive ranking of most four-year colleges and universities in the nation. It was not a simple compilation of good colleges; it was a regimented ranking, from number one on down.

This was not a new idea. Attempts have been made to rank colleges for more than a century, but most of those systems focused on individual academic departments or other specialized parts of a college or university. Predictably, they were interesting only to other educators. *U.S. News* broadened the approach by ranking whole institutions and publishing the results in a special annual issue. What a brilliant

> *Nearly a half million copies of the first issue sold and by the late 1990s U.S. News was printing more than 2.3 million copies. Sales were so good staff began referring to it as their "swimsuit issue."*

move it turned out to be! Nearly a half million copies of the first issue sold and by the late 1990s *U.S. News* was printing more than 2.3 million copies. Sales were so good staff began referring to it as their "swimsuit issue."

Don't Fall for Gimmicks

Predictably, the success of *U.S. News* spawned a variety of copycat efforts in the publishing world. *Newsweek* partnered with Kaplan Testing Service to produce its own annual guide. The Princeton Review published its own version. *Money* magazine later threw its hat into the mix.

Researcher Patricia McDonough of UCLA, who has studied the growth and impact of the ranking industry, estimated that by the end of the decade about 6.7 million copies of newsmagazine college rankings or guides were being sold each year. Even more were distributed free of charge. Total sales were estimated to be approximately $15 million, not including advertising revenue.

Since her study, the industry has grown only larger. There are specialty guides to the "most wired colleges" and to colleges that "encourage character development." There are lists of cheap colleges, most conservative colleges, most liberal colleges, and most disability friendly colleges. In such an aggressive, self-promoting business, publishers try to find new ways to nab a student's attention. It's possible to locate both "jock schools" and institutions populated by "dodgeball targets." There are colleges where "professors get high marks" and others where "professors suck all life out of materials." Both "bleeding heart liberals" and "stone cold conservatives" will find a place to call home.

Faced with these kinds of attention-getting gimmicks, it is tempting to dismiss rankings. But after twenty years, there is strong evidence that rankings have become an important resource for many college-bound students, especially those who are choosing one of the nation's more selective colleges. A much-cited study by UCLA found that while *fewer than half* of all college-bound students pay attention to rankings, the *majority* of high-achieving students do. According to the study, nearly 60 percent of students with SAT scores between 1000 and 1300 considered ranking to be either somewhat or very important. The percentage jumped to nearly 80 percent for those with SAT scores over 1300.

For these students, rankings do play a role and the most influential is undoubtedly *U.S. News'* annual guide to "America's Best Colleges." It is now the single most influential ranking and the one that excites the most controversy.

> *When Yale University made a relatively modest dip in the* U.S. News *ratings one year, from first to third place in the list of national universities, admissions staff predicted a 5 percent drop in applications and a 10 percent drop in campus visits.*

When Yale University—a solid, brand-name institution by any measurement—made a relatively modest dip in the *U.S. News* ratings one year, from first to third place in the list of national universities, admissions staff predicted a 5 percent drop in applications and a 10 percent drop in campus visits. Applications to Reed College in Oregon dropped a full 20 percent the year its president refused, *on principle*, to supply *U.S. News* with the data it needed to calculate the rankings. The magazine reportedly punished Reed that year by dropping the college from its first tier rating to the very bottom quarter. As a result, prospective students stayed away from Reed in droves.

We're Number One

Rankings are presented as friends of the student, impartial guides to quality, and a kind of *Consumer Reports* of higher education, but since their inception, rankings have proven enormously controversial. While students are led to believe that they are

> *"I can't think of a worse reason to pick a college [than because it's ranked number one]."*

being given the necessary tools to separate the best from the rest, most educators see misleading gibberish. It's tempting to chalk all this up to sour grapes. After all, there can only be one "number one" college. But even among the elite—those who regularly place at or near the top—cynicism abounds. Should students go to a college because it's number one? "I can't think of a worse reason to pick a college," states Marlyn McGrath Lewis, director of undergraduate admissions at Harvard University, a college that frequently ranks at the top.

What accounts for this disconnect? How can something be viewed as a trusted resource by students yet be dismissed by nearly all educators, including those who actually benefit from its findings?

According to Arthur Rothkopf, president of Lafayette College in Pennsylvania, the ranking system fails, in part, because the numbers gathered by the newsmagazines are not reliable measurements of educational quality. "Some [of the indicators measured] are perfectly valid factors to look at and much of the data identifies things students want to know," he concedes. "But the aggregate number—the number that generates its ranking— is inherently flawed. It is useful to know the range of SAT scores necessary for admission. It's also good to know the percentage of classes with enrollments of fifty or fewer. But the logic of the system falls apart when these numbers are combined and used to pass judgment on the institution's overall quality. Putting them together is necessarily arbitrary." Rothkopf questions why these ten or fifteen factors measure quality more reliably than another combination of factors. What would happen if a category was removed or existing categories were given greater or less weight? Even minor tinkering with the formula—which *U.S. News* does from time to time—produces a dramatic realignment of the list.

Consider the rise and fall of the California Institute of Technology (Caltech). For many years, this rigorous and selective institution ranked high, but never broke the Ivy League juggernaut. Then a new director of data, Amy Graham, joined *U.S. News*. Examining the magazine's ranking methodology, she saw a built-in bias toward Harvard, Princeton, and Yale. As a result, the magazine shifted the weights for a few categories in which several other institutions, such as Caltech, happened to excel. Suddenly, Caltech shot to the top of the list. A year later Graham left and the ranking formula was changed back. Princeton returned to the top and Caltech once again achieved a respectable, but middle-of-the-pack, ranking.

Officially, *U.S. News* says it is continually working to come up with a system that more accurately gauges excellence in higher education. But others have charged that the magazine's editors are purposely stacking the deck in favor of the Ivy League.

> *Caltech's days in the number one spot were numbered because it is an institution "where no* U.S. News *editors went."*

After leaving *U.S. News*, Graham coauthored an exposé of the magazine's ranking methodology. She charged that it is no accident that categories are weighted in ways that favor Harvard, Princeton, and Yale. After all, these are the alma maters of key magazine editors.

"Is this deliberate favoritism?" coauthor Nicholas Thompson was asked in a subsequent National Public Radio interview. "Oh, that's absolutely certain," he responded. Caltech's days in the number one spot were numbered because it is an institution "where no *U.S. News* editors went."

Going for a Ride

The point is not just that rankings may be biased toward the Ivy League. A scale that favors Caltech is not inherently more accurate or even fairer. It's simply another way to add the numbers. Instead, the story of Caltech illustrates the inherent weakness of any numerical ranking system, argue college presidents across the country. "The fundamental concept is flawed," charges Rothkopf. "It's not meaningful to rate colleges the same way you would athletic teams. It's just not so simple. My guess is you wouldn't find a college president in the country who would disagree with that."

Indeed, all presidents have experience with the inherently capricious nature of ranking systems that bounce their institutions up and down like a bungee cord. From one year to the next, most colleges and universities move at least a point up or down in the rankings and some take stomach-churning rides.

> *"The fundamental concept is flawed. It's not meaningful to rate colleges the same way you would athletic teams. It's just not so simple. My guess is you wouldn't find a college president in the country who would disagree with that."*

Many institutions have dropped as many as ten places in a single year, only to move up by nearly an equal number the following year. In a few cases, an institution strongly placed in the second tier one year found itself in the fourth tier a year later.

A few years ago, Gerhard Casper, former president of Stanford University, tracked the movement of his and other institutions over several years. He concluded "rankings lead readers to believe either that a university quality pops up and down like politicians in polls, or that last year's rankings were wrong but this year's are right." In a letter to *U.S. News*, he continued: "What else is one to make of Harvard being #1 one year and #3 the next, or Northwestern leaping in a single bound from #13 to #9? And it is not just this year. Could

Johns Hopkins be the twenty-second best national university two years ago, the tenth best last year, and the fifteenth best this year? Which is correct, that Columbia is #9 (two years ago), #15 (last year), or #11 (this year)?"

Presidents know more than most people that their institutions don't change much from year to year. Even with concerted effort, change usually occurs incrementally and is implemented at something approaching glacial speed. That's simply the nature of bureaucratic and administratively conservative institutions. Revolution is rare and continuity is the norm. From one year to the next, colleges retain most of their same faculty, teach the same courses, have about the same financial reserves, and attract a similar crop of students. The campus, as viewed by the president, the faculty, and students, looks much the same from one year to the next.

When an institution is on the move—for better or worse—it can take years for the changes to become obvious even to those on campus. In real life, the insignificant fluctuations that take place from year to year do not have any meaningful impact on the relative quality of the education students receive.

Cooking the Books

The presumed importance of rankings has produced one of the most persistent criticisms of rankings: cheating—or what Rothkopf calls "cooking the books." In the false precision of *U.S. News'* ranking formula, even small improvements in a college's admission yield, financial resources, or average SAT score can move a college or university up the list. This may give the college a small, but important, competitive advantage and help the college truly become a hot school or at least a slightly hotter school.

For the first ten years, *U.S. News* did little to verify the accuracy of the numbers reported by colleges, and an alarming number of institutions failed to live up to this kind of honor system. In 1992, the communications director of a small liberal arts college in Maine stumbled on the benefits of misrepresentation when he accidentally misreported the percentage of incoming freshmen who were in the top 10 percent of their high school classes. He told *U.S. News* it was an impressive 80 percent. The real number was 60 percent.

That error happened to push the college up five places in the rankings, but it also created a new dilemma. An accurate report the next year would produce an alarming *drop* in the rankings. What to do? This time, the communications director was *forced* to deliberately falsify some other data, inflating the amount of money spent per student on education, which indeed helped to sustain the college's forward march.

In 1995, Rothkopf sponsored a national conference among colleges and publishers of college guides to discuss the system. Unfortunately, little has changed since then, he argues. Admissions staffs, the very people who have the most at stake in the ratings game, are usually responsible for compiling data requested by *U.S. News*. It's their job to promote the college and bring in qualified applicants. Since a college's ranking will either help or hinder its work, the

"Fudging" has become a way of life for far too many institutions.

temptation to make the institution look as good as possible is understandably strong. Outright fabrication of data may be less common but, cautions Rothkopf, "There's a lot of game playing out there," especially in the reporting of admissions data. There are ways to increase the number of applications and ways to make the applicants look smarter than they really are.

According to Robert L. Woodbury, former chancellor of the University of Maine system, "fudging" has become a way of life for far too many institutions. A common strategy, he writes, is to encourage an unnecessarily large number of students to apply—far more than is needed to fill the freshman class. This allows the college or university to increase its rejection rate and, in this way, look like a more selective school. Another technique is to tinker with course schedules to produce either very large or very small classes. This improves the reported student/faculty ratio. These strategies are cynical and corrupting, Woodbury charges, but they are widespread.

Real or Reputation?

For all their numerical precision, most rankings are based on highly subjective information. In the *U.S. News* rankings, one quarter of a school's final score is based on its "reputation."

"A good reputation doesn't just happen," said one university official, quoted in the *Chronicle of Higher Education*. "When you do good things, you need to communicate them . . . or it's like they never happened."

Every year, *U.S. News* mails out surveys to college presidents to ask them to evaluate other colleges in the same category. (Presidents of national liberal arts colleges rate other liberal arts colleges, for example, while regional institutions critique other institutions in that region.) It seems reasonable. Fellow educators—those presumably most knowledgeable about higher education—should know better than the rest of us which colleges pass muster. But consider what *U.S. News* is *really* asking presidents to do. Those who head national liberal arts colleges must evaluate approximately 220 institutions from Maine to California, from North Dakota to Florida. Well-traveled presidents may indeed be familiar with a wide range of institutions, but they are not omniscient. Despite ten years as a top administrator, Rothkopf acknowledges he has "no clue" how to answer the surveys that are mailed each year. "For two thirds of the colleges, I simply say I don't know. These are the schools I know nothing about."

What about the rest? His responses about the seventy or eighty remaining institutions are based on what he admits is a grab bag of incomplete and often outdated impressions.

"I'm sort of an old guy so I may know a college from years ago. But I never visited the campus; I don't really know anything about

Rankings do not establish reputations as much as they reinforce them.

it. Or in some cases I know the president and I say, 'Oh, gee, that's a real good president.' But that's not a good reason. I think one of the best presidents I know is [from a college] in the middle of the pack. A great person. Does a great job. But as for his school, all I know is its admissions selectivity."

Once a college is known to be "good," even presidents have a hard time going against conventional wisdom. Indeed, a strong reputation is beguiling because it leads people to believe they "know" an institution even when all they really know is its reputation. "I don't know anything about Amherst," Rothkopf says. "I've never been there. But they are at the top [of the rankings]. So they must be good, right? So I put Amherst at the top. I could say I don't know, but how could I say that about Amherst? It's a great school."

Rothkopf's candor reveals what is easily missed in a ranking system that has a veneer of objectivity and scientific precision and is the single greatest problem with the industry: rankings do not *establish* reputations as much as they *reinforce* them.

From the "Best" College to the Right College

Prospective students who are lured to top-ranked schools only because they are considered the "best" do themselves a tremendous disservice.

College rankings distort the truth about college admissions. They create a false impression that there are very few good colleges.

These students often become the victims of a capricious and cynical marketing strategy that delivers the opposite of what it promises. Instead of measuring a college or university's quality, it focuses on unstable and superficial substitutes—usually reputation and selectivity. Instead of giving students confidence, it promotes uncertainty and stress as students try to squeeze into the handful of brand-name institutions. Instead of empowering students with knowledge and confidence, it encourages a passive attitude. Too many students approach the college admissions process with the attitude, "Tell me who *you* want me to be and I'll be that person."

College rankings distort the truth about college admissions. They create a false impression that there are very few good colleges. Yet educators—even at top-ranked schools— know that this is not true. Marlyn McGrath Lewis is adamant in her assertion that "there are literally hundreds of good colleges and universities." Could this statement be dismissed as false modesty from a top-ranked institution? "No, I'm serious," she repeats.

When students consider a wider range of institutions, they can worry less about being part of the 80 or 90 percent who are rejected from the most highly selective of the top-ranked institutions. If nothing else, prospective students should remember this: most colleges, including many well-respected institutions, accept the majority of students who apply. When I ask college-bound students to guess what percentage of college applicants are admitted to their first-choice school, the most common answer is "10 percent." The truth is that in 2001, *70 percent* of students gained entry into their first-choice school, and another 22 percent were studying at their second-choice school. To a degree most students don't appreciate, *they* are in control of the college admissions process.

This knowledge is the key to real confidence and empowerment in the college search process. Knowing that prospective students have many options, that "quality" exists across the spectrum of higher education, and that there is no one "best" school is the first step in taking the stress out of the college choice process. In a nation where most people now enroll in college at some point during their lives, diversity of higher education options exists for a reason. In order to find the *right* school, students need to keep their options open and consider all of the available paths to a college degree.

Finding the *right fit* need not be a process of random investigation. Rather than immediately focusing on particular institutions, the college search should begin by exploring different kinds of colleges. Knowing that there are large universities and small colleges, as well as public and private, is only the first step. Different categories of institutions have fundamentally different histories, different missions, and different campus climates. Understanding the rich menu of options in the savvy college search is the subject of the next chapter.

When students pick the right kind of college, they are ready to take the next step and compare institutions. Although rankings do a poor job of identifying what really matters in a college education, there are meaningful differences among institutions. Knowing how to select the right college or university is not hard when the right questions are asked. Getting beyond the college tour happy talk and "three under a tree" viewbook photos is simply a matter of focusing on a few key criteria of quality, what matters in college education, and what questions to ask.

why not harvard?

Jim Nickovich didn't worry much about finding the right college. "To be honest, in my senior year of high school I was busy playing football, basketball, and trying to have fun with my friends," he admits. "The college search wasn't at the forefront." Still, the decision to attend college was never in doubt. "It was always in the background, and my parents didn't push it too much. They knew I would end up in school and allowed me to figure it out for myself."

Taking the lead in the college search process, Jim began looking for a school that was compatible with his personality and interests. "In high school I was outspoken. I liked having discussions. I liked talking directly to the teacher," he recalls. "Part of my goal was to find a college with small classrooms where I'd be able to interact with professors. That was definitely at the top of the list."

Jim also wanted a college that was friendly and where he could play on the football team. "I also wanted to have a good time socially. I wanted a place where I could make friends and experience the college environment, where I could have a good time and have things to do." Cost was a key issue, too. He needed a college that would offer him scholarships.

During the early part of his college search, he visited colleges in the Southeast. But when it came time to apply, he settled on schools closer to home. Letters of acceptance came back from five colleges and universities. It was a diverse assortment of institutions ranging from Wabash College, a small liberal arts college in Indiana, to the University of Chicago, a large urban university. He chose something in between—Butler University, a comprehensive university in Indiana. What put this school over the top?

"What I found was that a lot of the schools [I visited] had small classrooms and offered a quality education, but there wasn't much to do socially. I wanted that balance . . . social gatherings and a good education."

A dozen other factors surrounded this careful comparison of academic strengths and social opportunities. He could play football. He was offered scholarships. His high school coach recommended it. It was the right distance from home. He was aggressively pursued by the university's admissions office. And finally, there was a *feeling* that it was the right place. When asked to describe the deciding factor—the one thing that mattered more than any other—Jim talks about the intangible qualities of friendliness and aesthetics.

"As I walked around the campus, people were extremely friendly. It was an aesthetically pleasing environment. When I sat in on classes, I really felt that I was more than just a number. I was a person. I weighed all these things and knew this was the school I was looking for."

After four years, Jim knows he made the right choice. Although he didn't know what he wanted to study, he knew he wanted a place that would give him a chance to grow and explore his options. Open to new experiences, he spent a semester studying in London and, following his academic interests, he double-majored in English and history. Jim now looks forward to continuing his education and is leaning toward a career in law.

In many ways, Jim tells a common story. Like a growing number of high school graduates, he took college for granted; he didn't have a specific career path in mind but did believe that, whatever the future might hold, a college degree would be useful. And, like many 18-year-olds, he looked forward to independence and new experiences.

Jim also followed a predictable path. He narrowed his search around schools closer to home, listened to the recommendations of people he respected, and considered all of the scholarship opportunities. He also selected schools that were strong both academically and socially. Satisfied that all of his top contenders met these criteria, Jim followed his heart when it was time to make his final decision. He picked the school that was friendly and had a great campus; a place, he admitted, that satisfied *his* image of what a college should be.

Jim is happy he chose Butler. He thrived academically and built a strong foundation for graduate school and a promising career. What is the lesson to be drawn from Jim's story? Is it that everyone should be like Jim and enroll at Butler or a college just like it? Before jumping to conclusions, consider the experience of another student, who also knows she made the right choice and, like Jim, is on the fast track to success.

Explore Your Options

Kate McGlew graduated from high school as a bright and intellectually curious young woman. However, despite their similarities, Jim and Kate chose two very different paths.

"I knew I wasn't ready for college right out of high school so I got a job right away." Her parents were disappointed and, as a compromise, she agreed to enroll part-time at nearby Asnuntuck Community College in Connecticut. "They really encouraged me to start taking classes, just one class a semester."

She didn't mind going to the community college but she lacked direction and felt uninspired. "It was kind of like going to high school all over again," she recalls. "I just wasn't motivated." She persisted for several years with this kind of part-time, on-again, off-again education. "I did well in some classes, didn't do well in others. I wasn't very serious about it."

But then something changed. After living away from home for several years and advancing about as far as she could in her job as a retail manager, Kate began comparing her life to that of her peers. "I had that reality check with my high school reunion coming up. It got me in gear and I said to myself, 'I can do so much better than this.'" She decided to make education a priority. Friends encouraged her to apply to selective liberal arts colleges, especially Smith College and Mount Holyoke College, both in Massachusetts. But she wasn't ready for a four-year school just yet.

Looking back, Kate blames her early ambivalence about college and lackluster grades on a lack of confidence. "For me, it was a huge fear of failure issue. Even in high school and the first few classes I took at Asnuntuck, I was afraid to put in the effort because everyone was telling me how smart I was and how I could do anything. But I really didn't believe it. I thought, 'If I really try and I fail, people are going to realize that I'm not so smart.'"

But through maturity and a sense of purpose, Kate returned to Asnuntuck and became a completely different student. With admission to Smith or another liberal arts college as her goal, she became a top student and appreciated all the community college had to offer. "When I was young

"When I was young and all my friends were going off to college, it was embarrassing to say that I was 'only' going to the community college. Now I have a completely different perspective."

and all my friends were going off to college, it was embarrassing to say that I was 'only' going to the community college. Now I have a completely different perspective. I can look at the college for the great services it provides."

At a time when she needed to build up her confidence, she thrived in the supportive atmosphere that Asnuntuck provided. "There are really fabulous professors who really help you out. There aren't great big lecture halls with 200 students, and a professor lecturing from the front. There are small classes, maybe twenty-five people in a class. And all the teachers know the situation their students are in, and they're all very approachable."

She enrolled in classes that will allow her to transition to three selective liberal arts colleges. Her top choice is Smith, which has a special program for older students. But her goal now extends far beyond a four-year degree. Kate plans to earn a Ph.D. in American Literature and teach at a college—maybe a community college.

Jim and Kate have a lot in common. They are both bright, articulate, and outgoing and clearly enjoy the challenge of learning. Both have made the most of their college experiences. Jim arrived at Butler not knowing what he wanted to study but confident that he couldn't go wrong if he followed his intellectual interests. "I just took what interested me the most and would provide me with the best grades and the best opportunities," he says. For her part, Kate wasn't committed to higher education until she gained confidence and a clear sense of direction. But once a path opened up, she made the most of her college experience.

For Jim, opportunities and expectations led him to college right after high school. Kate followed another route. Yet, both are clearly happy with their choices and feel that they have picked schools that meet their special needs. Neither feels penalized by his or her choice. Indeed, they both are grateful to their respective institutions and know they contributed to their success and self-confidence.

Many Paths to Success

The experiences of Jim and Kate suggest that there is no one "right" route through college. Kate wasn't ready for a place like Butler University. Jim never considered a community college. Both found that their own choices worked for them and, because they were happy, success followed. These different paths create different opportunities and challenges, but they exist for a reason.

Jim and Kate, as different as they are, both felt welcomed and successful in college because American higher education is large and diverse and—especially in recent years—provides new paths for learning. More than ever, colleges bend over backward to serve the needs and interests of students. Like a diner, the door is always open, there are plenty of seats, and the menu is large and enticing.

Break Down Barriers

So many choices exist because there are so many colleges and universities—4,182 at last count. This number reflects the philosophy of a democratic nation. Education is believed to be the great equalizer, the path to advancement—not for the elite minority, but for all Americans of ambition. Not all who enter college succeed. In fact, more than half of those who enroll fail to graduate within the expected number of years. But if success is not guaranteed, the opportunity to at least try has become the right of all.

Of course, not all Americans benefit equally from higher education. Today, barriers still exist for those who lack money for tuition or are handicapped by a weak elementary and high school education. However, the *goal* of education in the modern era is inclusion, not exclusion, and the larger story of higher education is one of expanding opportunities for more and more Americans.

A Diverse Student Body

Historically, American colleges and universities have found ways to break down barriers and bring more students onto their campuses. What is taking place right now, however, is something new. Not only are more people enrolling in college but colleges and universities are transforming themselves radically to attract a new population of students. As more Americans go to college, they are rewriting the old rules of higher education. Everyone, even the "typical" 18-year-old college freshman, is affected by these changes.

> *Not only are more people enrolling in college but colleges are transforming themselves radically to attract a new population of students.*

American higher education has experienced several periods of rapid expansion. The roots of this modern revolution began about twenty-five years ago when colleges and universities were facing a crisis. For twenty years they had grown fat and happy on a postwar baby boom generation that began rolling into college and university campuses in the 1960s. The number of 18-year-olds enrolling in college climbed by nearly a quarter of a million between 1970 and 1980.

By the late 1980s, the number of 18-year-olds enrolling in college had decreased by well over a quarter of a million. Researchers predicted a significant drop in college enrollments for years to come. Schools would face tough competition for students. Some predicted that dozens, even hundreds, of colleges would close.

However, a funny thing happened. Even as the number of 18-year-olds dropped precipitously, the total number of Americans enrolling in college actually *increased*. According to the *Chronicle 2002 Almanac*, over the past forty years, the number of Americans attending college has climbed from about 6 million in 1965, to 12 million in 1985 and, finally, to nearly 15 million in 2002.

Many of these students were minorities, women, and "nontraditional" students, especially older students and part-time learners. Today, about one third of all students in higher education are older than 24 and 40 percent complete their degrees part-time. The "typical" college student—a young adult studying full-time at a residential college—is the minority.

The growth in the number of nontraditional students is explained, in part, by the willingness—even eagerness— of American colleges and universities to attract new students and satisfy their diverse needs and interests.

As more diverse students enroll in college, higher education must become more flexible and student-centered.

When the supply of 18-year-olds ran low, colleges and universities opened doors to millions of Americans who, in an earlier era, never would have considered college. Weekend classes, evening courses and, increasingly, online classes became accepted paths to a degree. Community colleges also came into their own. In fact, today, well over one third of all students are enrolled in two-year institutions.

As more diverse students enroll in college—18-year-olds fresh out of high school, professionals seeking a second (or third) career, single moms looking for employable skills, among many others—higher education must become more flexible and student-centered. Thus, colleges and universities now offer more degrees, more convenient schedules, and new services.

As a result of this student-centered system of education, the college experience is responsive to the needs and interests of its students. This trend has good points and bad points, but the bottom line is that students can set the terms of their education. How, when, and where students study is determined by choice, not by rules or social conventions.

The Right Fit

Students need to understand their choices and find, as Jim and Kate did, "the right fit." Given so many choices, students' first step is to know what they want from higher education. So, before interviewing with college admissions counselors, they should ask themselves:

- *What do I expect the college experience to be like?* Is the traditional, residential college environment important? How important are social life and extra-curricular activities?

- *What barriers do I face?* Can my college career be sabotaged by a lack of funds, competing obligations (from family or work), lack of confidence, or poor academic preparation?

- *What do I want to get out of four or more years of learning?* Am I here to train for a specific career, or is a bachelor's degree the first step toward a graduate or professional degree?

These are fundamental questions, and the ability to answer each with confidence is critical to a successful college search. Yet, they are frequently overlooked. All too often, students take for granted the decision to go to college and neglect to think about what they hope to gain from the experience. But if these questions are not asked, and if students head off to a school that is "good" but doesn't satisfy their needs or interests, disappointment and possibly failure to complete the four-year term may result.

So, the goal is not simply to find an institution that is *good* but to find an institution that is a *good fit.* After all, getting into college is only the first step (and not as hard as many students think). What really matters is not the letter of acceptance but what happens over the next four or more years.

Valparaiso University President Alan Harre drives this point home whenever he speaks to prospective students

visiting his campus.
"What matters in the
end is whether or not
you as the student fit

Finding the right fit is really what the college search is all about.

the institution that you're going to attend. What you need to know is that each college or university is what it is. We're not going to change for you. You're going to have to determine what you want to be and how you're going to live your life and then figure out which [institution] comes closest to that."

Finding the *right fit* is really what the college search is all about. But with so many choices, the task can seem overwhelming. It is, of course, impossible to evaluate more than 4,000 institutions. To cut down the list of potential institutions to a manageable number, students are often advised to make their "first cut" based on a few broad criteria, such as cost, size, selectivity, and location. Quick answers to these questions early in the selection process can whittle down the number of contenders.

Frequently, assumptions about the cost of higher education play a role in deciding where to focus your college search. Prospective students often reject private institutions based on the assumption that they will not be affordable. Likewise, assumptions about quality often play a role. For those who believe that only the "best" schools can be the right school, nothing but a highly-ranked institution will suffice.

It certainly simplifies the process to decide, for example, even before taking a single campus tour, that only state

> *A savvy college search should be built around a strategy that opens up doors, not one that shuts down options.*

schools in the West or schools at the top of the rankings will be considered. And, in the end, these schools might be the right choice. But premature decisions based *only* on cost or reputation have little to do with finding colleges that are good fits. A savvy college search should be built around a strategy that opens up doors, not one that shuts down options.

Where to Begin

Bobby Fong, president of Butler University, has some recommendations. He is a father who has sent several children to college. Although he's proud of his institution and has many good things to say about the quality of its education, he knows that it's not necessarily the right choice for everyone—not even his own children. Like thousands of other parents across the country, he recently accompanied his youngest son, John, on a whirlwind tour of colleges.

Before they left, he offered John some advice. He urged him not to make hasty judgments about the colleges he was visiting. Instead, he wanted him to explore the strengths of different kinds of colleges. "My basic suggestion was that we're going to hit nine institutions in five days; don't concentrate on analyzing why you liked or didn't like a given institution. Get a sense of the institutions and, at the end of the trip, let's look at what the institutions that made a favorable impression on you had in common."

Fong continued: "That's what John did and, as a result, he returned home with some well-informed ideas about the kind of school he wanted. At the end of our tour he decided that he really wanted a smaller place that emphasized faculty/student contact, had high academic standards, and offered opportunities for study abroad. In addition, he preferred a place without private societies [fraternities and sororities] and used that criterion to narrow a tentative list we had made up."

John's mother took him on another tour of colleges in the East. This time, he focused his search on small liberal arts colleges. "He fell in love with Connecticut College," Fong says, and the whole process ended happily, without undo stress or second guessing. "He applied and got in. We were through our travails by December."

Finding the Right Kind of College

Fong isn't suggesting that all families follow in his son's footsteps, but as a long-time college president he knows a few things about higher education that most students and parents do not. For example, students fail to appreciate that colleges and universities can be divided into several distinct categories, and that different types of institutions offer different types of experiences. Most students and parents know, in general terms, that there are large universities and small colleges as well as public and private. Yet these distinctions, while real, only scratch the surface of what shapes the college experience. The differences between large and small schools, for example, reach far beyond the number of students on campus.

"I find that parents and students don't understand that there are real differences in the expectations for teaching and learning between liberal arts and research universities," explains Fong. Rather than visiting institutions randomly, it's best to know what kind of college you are considering and be aware of the traits unique to that kind of institution.

Common Traits

Research Universities

This category is, at first glance, large and diverse. It ranges from private Ivy League institutions like Princeton to the so-called "public Ivies" like the University of Virginia. There are also state universities that are, in some cases, more famous for their football teams than for the number of Nobel laureates they have educated. Public or private, many are quite large and, in fact, eight universities now enroll more than 40,000 students and the nation's largest, the University of Texas at Austin, enrolls nearly 50,000 students.

What distinguishes these institutions from the rest is not the number of enrollments but their history and mission. The image many Americans hold today of universities as centers of scientific discovery can be traced back to the late nineteenth century when they began importing and adapting the German university model. At that time, Germany was making great advances in the sciences through what we now consider to be the typical scientist—a scholar conducting exhaustive research in a university laboratory and sharing his or her findings in scholarly journals.

Of course, "science" also existed in the United States but it was, according to historian Laurence Veysey, a more informal "homegrown" variety. In contrast, the German model valued knowledge for its own sake and became part of university life.

When Americans brought this understanding of science back home and grafted it onto their universities, they redefined the mission and priorities of their institutions. By 1918, the influential sociologist Thorstein Veblen defined the American university as "a body of mature scholars and scientists, the 'faculty'—with whatever plant and other equipment may incidentally serve as appliances for their work." In other words, the university was presented as nothing more than a group of scientists surrounded by the equipment necessary to complete research—labs, test tubes, heating ducts, and electric lights.

Look again at Veblen's definition and notice what is conspicuously absent—students and teaching! The glorification of pure science produced an explosion of new knowledge but it also created institutions that, for the first time in America, marginalized both undergraduate teaching and undergraduate students.

The impact of this transformation is still felt today on university campuses across the nation. Undergraduates make up the majority of students in nearly every institution, yet many professors admit that teaching is not their top priority—not because they dislike

> *Undergraduates make up the majority of students in nearly every institution, yet many professors admit that teaching is not their top priority.*

teaching (most say they value teaching) but because good teaching is not rewarded as much as good research. A professor who publishes influential articles in scholarly journals is praised and promoted more quickly than a professor who refines his or her skills as a teacher. A recent survey by the Carnegie Foundation found that 95 percent of faculty members believe it is either fairly important or very important to publish scholarly articles in order to advance in their careers. In contrast, only about 50 percent believe it is equally important to receive good student evaluations.

When prospective students visit research universities and see a campus dominated by undergraduates, it's easy to forget that there is another side to academic life. But they feel it indirectly. With large enrollments, limited budgets (especially at state-supported universities), and different priorities, most undergraduate teaching is handed off to graduate students and part-time instructors who are grossly underpaid and have no clout within their institutions.

The undergraduate curriculum may suffer in other ways. Universities are organized around different branches of knowledge—the "disciplines" of science, the arts, and the humanities, to name a few broad categories. Faculty members tend to be most loyal to their discipline and generally interact only with other faculty members and students who are interested in their subject. Engineers hang out with engineers and tend to think of themselves as engineers, not faculty members of a particular university. This means that relatively little attention is paid to undergraduate education and, in particular, to general education—the broad, introductory liberal arts courses that shape the core of an undergraduate student's education.

As a result, many undergraduates get bounced around from department to department during their first two years of college as they fulfill "distribution requirements." The argument is that students will be exposed to the breadth and richness of knowledge by taking a sampling of elective courses "distributed" throughout the university curriculum—a few courses in English, some in history, some in the sciences, and some in the arts. Each is taught as an introductory class by the different departments. Yet no real effort is made to pull all this knowledge together. Rather, it is up to the students to pick a meaningful selection of courses and connect the intellectual dots.

On the other hand, research universities have advantages that other colleges do not. Their size and comprehensive mission mean that students have many educational options. Students pursue traditional liberal arts degrees in English, history, philosophy, and the arts, among others, while many other students pursue an ever-expanding array of career-oriented degrees in everything from

More promising is a growing movement within research universities to deal with their limitations and build on their strengths.

business to the culinary arts. Like large cities, large universities are more diverse and offer a richer array of extracurricular options. For many students, this more than compensates for the size and rigidity of the curriculum.

More promising is a growing movement within research universities to deal with their limitations and build on their strengths. Some universities pay more attention to their general education programs, and one of the newest movements is to find ways to include undergraduates in the research process. Rather than excluding students from labs, a few are finding ways to enrich teaching by encouraging students to participate in the work of top researchers.

Liberal Arts Colleges

Liberal arts colleges are the opposite of large research universities. The most obvious difference is size. Liberal arts colleges typically have enrollments in the low thousands. They are usually residential colleges and, in most cases, nearly all students study full-time. This makes them an attractive option for students looking for a cozier, less intimidating, and more nurturing college experience. Like research universities, liberal arts colleges are defined by more than the number of students they enroll. They also have their own set of values and expectations.

Although liberal arts colleges reflect the most venerable tradition of higher education—preparing students to be wise thinkers and informed citizens—they have to defend themselves against criticism that they are not sufficiently practical.

Liberal arts colleges represent the oldest and most enduring tradition of higher education in America, providing undergraduate students with broad exposure to a liberal arts curriculum. "Liberal arts," in the academic sense, refers to the core knowledge of society—its history, languages, philosophy, and art, among other areas. It is *not* the study of professional and vocational subjects. Thus, English is a proper liberal arts major, but journalism is not. In this sense, students who graduate from a liberal arts college are "broadly" educated, although generally not for any particular career.

With few or no graduate programs, teaching is the preeminent role of faculty at liberal arts colleges. Research is valued (increasingly so, by some accounts), but it is not the most important measure of success among faculty. Good teaching is both expected and valued. This philosophy, combined with their smaller size, means that most classes are smaller and are usually taught by full-time faculty. Even required introductory courses are often small enough to be taught as interactive seminars and led by a senior member of the faculty. One-on-one attention from faculty, both in and out of the classroom, is usually presented as the key advantage of a liberal arts college.

Although liberal arts colleges reflect the most venerable tradition of higher education—preparing students to be wise thinkers and informed citizens—they have to defend themselves against criticism that they are not sufficiently practical. At a time when most students come to college because it is a necessary route to a job, many ask: "What is the value of a history degree?" or "Who will hire me to be a philosopher?"

However, advocates of liberal arts education respond that this kind of broad training is relevant. That's what Shirley Kenny, president of Stony Brook University, State University of New York, argues. "It really doesn't matter what you major in," she contends. "It's what you learn and how you learn to put it together. It's learning to ask the right questions. It needs to be intellectually stimulating."

But there is tacit acknowledgment that a liberal arts degree—whether from a small college or large university—is not sufficient qualification for a growing number of careers. Its value is providing the broad intellectual foundation and critical-thinking skills needed to succeed in graduate school.

The advanced or professional degree will then give the qualifications needed for many careers.

Kenny agrees. Students and parents "really need to think of undergraduate education not as professional qualification because, in so many ways, it's the graduate degree that professionally qualifies you. For example, if you want to be in business, you're probably better off having a degree in the arts and sciences and then getting an M.B.A."

Comprehensive Colleges

Liberal arts colleges and research universities represent two extremes. But there is a broad middle ground filled with institutions that reflect some of the qualities of both. These are known as "comprehensive colleges." These institutions are committed to both undergraduate teaching and a liberal arts curriculum while also offering an assortment of professional degrees—often in business, nursing, and education, to name a few.

Comprehensive colleges may be public or private and range widely in enrollments. According to Bobby Fong, what distinguishes comprehensive colleges from their liberal arts counterparts are the expectations of students. "The difference for many students who come to Butler is that their parents are willing to underwrite a private education for four years but may not have the means to continue to underwrite a graduate school education. In short, they need a job after receiving their baccalaureate degree. So what we have in a comprehensive teaching university like Butler is the opportunity both to be liberally educated in fairly small classroom situations and to obtain a professional degree."

In other words, comprehensive colleges and universities position themselves as institutions that offer both the breadth and richness of a liberal arts college and the utility of a research university. The betwixt and between mission of comprehensive colleges is often hard to summarize in concise ways, acknowledges Fong, who counts Butler as a comprehensive institution. "Unfortunately, I haven't gotten it down to a one-sentence sound bite," he admits.

> *Comprehensive colleges and universities position themselves as institutions that offer both the breadth and richness of a liberal arts college and the utility of a research university.*

Most comprehensive colleges are categorized as "regional" institutions, which means that most students come from within state or neighboring states. At their best, these colleges are also regional in the sense that they respond to the needs of the communities they serve. Belmont University in Tennessee, for example, takes advantage of its proximity to Nashville by offering a commercial music program. Others colleges and universities may have especially strong connections to the local government, schools, and business community that are useful for students who hope to enrich their classroom experiences with internships and service projects.

Community Colleges

Community colleges can be the butt of jokes among nervous high school students. "If I don't get into Berkeley, well, there's always a community college." But the truth is that community colleges are among the fastest growing and most dynamic of all colleges in the United States. As the new kids on the block, community colleges are less than 100 years old. They expanded in the 1950s when they were viewed as institutions for

Community colleges are among the fastest growing and most dynamic of all colleges in the United States.

people who would not, or could not, succeed in a four-year college. With a strictly vocational program, they offered high school graduates an opportunity to get some specialized training for work in fields ranging from carpentry to secretarial science.

But, in recent years, community colleges have expanded their scope and, in a remarkable new trend, have begun to attract students who not long ago would have considered only a four-year college or university. For these students, community colleges offer transfer programs that fulfill general education requirements before transferring to a four-year institution.

Economics plays a role in this trend. As college costs rise, public community colleges remain the least expensive route to higher education, both because tuition is generally less and because students usually live at home while they take classes. But many other factors help to fuel the trend. Community colleges have earned praise for their commitment to teaching. Like liberal arts colleges, teaching is the first priority of faculty, and classes are usually small, even in required subjects.

In recent years, community colleges have also benefited from the tight job market for college faculty. Newly minted Ph.D.s—especially in the humanities—often have a hard time finding teaching positions at four-year colleges and universities. Some are turning to community colleges—often by necessity—but increasingly by choice. They also appreciate the opportunity to work at a college where teaching is a priority and allows for greater interaction between students and teachers.

> *More than any other type of institution, community colleges are dedicated to diversity.*

More than any other type of institution, community colleges are dedicated to diversity. They are nonselective institutions, admitting anyone with a high school diploma or a high school equivalency diploma. This enriches the classroom experience in many ways. Class discussions that incorporate the experiences of 18-year-olds and retirees are unlike anything experienced in most traditional college class-rooms.

Conversely, because they are nonselective, community colleges have the highest noncompletion rates of any college. Some students find they are not ready for college or can't fit classes into their busy lives. And not all students plan to earn a degree. Many simply want to take classes for personal enrichment. In either case, it means that dedicated students usually find that many of their peers are less committed or less prepared. A high turnover rate also diminishes a sense of community that many traditional undergraduates desire. And because most community colleges are nonresidential and serve people who also work or have family responsibilities, extracurricular life is often less vibrant. When class is over, most students go elsewhere.

Looking for Differences

Research universities, liberal arts colleges, comprehensive colleges, and community colleges provide different educational experiences and are the *right fit* for different kinds of students. But it is not always easy to discern these differences when looking at recruitment literature. There is a tendency among colleges and universities to downplay their distinctive missions. Instead, at the risk of alienating potential students, promotional literature, Web sites, and college tours often give the impression that every college and

university represents the very best qualities of all these different types of institutions.

Thus, a large research university may bend over backward
to show prospective students that they will receive personal
attention from teachers but will not discuss how much time
these scholars spend in the laboratory or library compared to
the time they spend teaching. This doesn't mean that some
research universities are not sincerely trying to focus on the
needs of undergraduate students. However, viewbook photos
and rhetoric don't make it so.

In contrast, liberal arts colleges find themselves talking
more than they want to about how "practical" and "useful"
their programs are. While many educators feel uneasy about
trying to justify the value of a rich undergraduate curriculum
only in terms of how much graduates will earn, they also know
that this is one of the most compelling arguments for many
students and families. "We have to justify the investment that
students and parents are making in higher education," says
Alan Harre. "On the one hand, we have to do that to get the
attention of students. But, at the same time, we are reinforc-
ing the stereotypes and the very attitudes with which we have
some major concerns." Yet, he acknowledges, "If we only talk
about the theoretical and the philosophical [value of higher
education] in this current environment, we won't get heard.
Our sound bites get lost in the millions of sound bites that
are out there because a lot of institutions are going to continue to talk the vocational language, even though they're also
going to say—in passing—they're interested in the liberal arts."

Ultimately, what is happening is an attempt to suggest that every college and university, despite their histories and missions, draws from both the liberal arts and research traditions. Research universities want to look as warm and cozy as grandma's

> *The smart college search is based on an understanding of the strengths and weaknesses of every type of college.*

home, while liberal arts colleges want to look as useful and cutting-edge as a research university. However, they are not the same, and the smart college search is based on an understanding of the strengths and weaknesses of every type of college.

Looking for Guarantees

For sure, there are different colleges and different students. But the temptation to pick a highly-ranked college is based partly on the belief that its reputation provides an added advantage in the marketplace. The perception is that those who go to highly-ranked institutions are more likely to get better paying jobs and advance more quickly in their chosen careers. This approach to college admissions focuses less on the college experience and more on the promise of economic rewards after graduation.

But is this true? Is the financial advantage so great that it should override other considerations when choosing a college? Not surprisingly, there has been a great deal of research done over the years assessing the link between a college degree and future earnings. Yet, despite all the research, the answer is, "It all depends." First, there is no guarantee that graduates of highly-selective institutions will be richer than those who follow other paths of higher education. As in everything else in life, success (as measured by income) depends on many factors, most of which are not connected to the type of college students attend. Family background, individual aspirations and ambitions, and the quality of one's early educational experiences are among the many factors that, collectively, are more powerful predictors of success. The world is filled with millionaires who never went to college. Conversely, the world is also filled with impoverished Ph.D.s. Go figure.

> *One of the strongest findings is that people who hold a college degree—any kind of college degree from any kind of institution—are statistically more likely to earn more than those who do not.*

That said, researchers do see patterns. One of the strongest findings is that people who hold a college degree—any kind of college degree from any kind of institution—are statistically more likely to earn more than those who do not. This finding only confirms what most Americans assume and can see in their own lives. Many jobs are open only to college graduates and, in some professions, opportunities for advancement are linked to one's education level.

According to the latest U.S. Census, a college graduate, over a lifetime, will earn almost twice as much as someone who only has a high school diploma—$2.1 million versus $1.2 million. Average lifetime earnings for someone with a master's degree climb to $2.5 million. A person holding a professional degree, such as medicine or law, earns an average of $4.4 million.

More education usually correlates to higher income, but not always. Graduates of community and technical colleges sometimes earn more because they have specialized training that qualifies them for in-demand jobs. A recent study published in the *Milwaukee Journal Sentinel* compared students who completed their education in several schools and colleges in the Milwaukee area and found that graduates of the local technical college with two-year degrees in fire science, refrigeration repair, or nurs-

College is not just about money; it's also about gaining confidence, wisdom, and a sense of place within the rich tapestry of human experience.

ing had average annual incomes exceeding $50,000. This number is quite a bit higher than graduates of the local state university who held four-year or professional degrees in such fields as architecture, criminal justice, or social work. In fact, in some regions, it appears that ambitious scholars are penalized for their education. A recent study published in the *Charleston Gazette* found that West Virginians who held an associate degree were actually earning more, on average, than residents who held either a bachelor's or a doc-toral degree.

These findings reinforce a central point: College is use-ful, but no one kind of college is the key to success. So does this mean that one college is as good as another, that there are no meaningful differences? Not at all. College is not just about money; it's also about gaining confidence, wisdom, and a sense of place within the rich tapestry of human experience. Growing as a person is, traditionally, not only a function of the undergraduate experience, but also the central justification for higher education. In this realm, not all colleges and universities are the same. Once pro-spective students examine their own needs and expectations and begin the college search, the next step is to look at those things that really do define quality.

chapter 3
what students really need to learn

Colleges and universities are becoming more flexible, more accommodating, and more innovative. Community colleges, distance learning courses, and evening and weekend programs all reflect this trend. But perhaps the most important changes are happening *inside* the classroom. Higher education is changing—sometimes radically—both in the way it teaches and what it wants students to learn.

The most forward-thinking colleges and universities know it is not enough to say students are "educated" because they have completed their courses and earned a degree. An institution that provides only a credential for entry-level employment is an institution that has failed. Graduates need more than a diploma. They need to be able to keep up with the changes that will inevitably take place both in their careers and in society. A quality institution helps students gain the wisdom and insight they need to become future leaders.

Learn How to Learn

This is a new way of thinking about the role of higher education, says Shirley Kenny, president of Stony Brook University, State University of New York. "When I was an undergraduate I really believed that if I could read every book in the university library, I would become a learned person. But there's no way you can read everything and, if you know the truth of two years ago, it's not today's truth because of new discoveries and new science."

According to Kenny, colleges and universities must respond to this new era, not by trying to cram more facts into the heads of students but by providing something far more useful. Quality institutions measure success through their ability to teach students how to think critically, communicate, understand ethical implications, and respond to the larger forces that shape the world around them.

President Kenny doesn't think students are "vessels that we can pour facts into and say they're educated. People thought that was possible in the eighteenth century, but that's not how we should deal with education today. Instead, students have to acquire the hunger for learning and the ability to pursue it."

A growing number of presidents agree. Loren Anderson, president of Pacific Lutheran University in Tacoma, Washington, makes almost the same point. "A college education," he says, "is not about storing up a body of knowledge that will

> *"All students will need to be nimble thinkers and creative problem solvers."*

provide you with the answers. Rather, it's about exposure to bodies of knowledge. Fundamentally, it's about irretrievably awakening students' curiosity about the world and then giving them the tools to allow them to go where their curiosity leads them. Of course, a college education equips students to get their first teaching job, pass the nurses licensing board exam, or get into the graduate school of their choice," he acknowledges. "But there's something happening here that is ultimately much more important."

According to the *Greater Expectations* report released by the Association of American Colleges and Universities (AAC&U), students need an education that prepares them for a knowledge-based economy and an interdependent world. The report argues that "all students will need to be nimble thinkers and creative problem solvers. To think outside the box, they will need to depend on intellectual flexibility, at least as much as on factual information."

Future Shock

For years educators have argued for a more flexible, experience-oriented approach to education. Indeed, the comments of Presidents Kenny and Anderson are similar to past critiques of education. In the midst of the social, technological, and political upheaval of the modern era, these critics argue that education at all levels must become more flexible, more adaptable, and more interdisciplinary.

For example, more than thirty years ago famed "futurist" Alvin Toffler argued for a system of education that reflected the changes taking place in modern society. He proposed that education should reflect an ever-changing society. In his bestseller, *Future Shock*, he wrote:

> In a modern superindustrial society we have not merely extended the scope and scale of change, we have radically altered its pace. We have in our time released a totally new social force—a stream of change so accelerated that it influences our sense of time, revolutionizes the tempo of daily life, and affects the way we feel about the world around us.

In a "future shock" world, the familiar is swept aside and is replaced with innovation, novelty, and revolutionary social change. These changes are unavoidable. However, Toffler warned that our ability to adapt is hampered by a philosophy of education more equipped for a nineteenth-century industrial society. Indeed, the current model of education—from elementary school to college—is based on the antiquated factory model. Toffler argued that "the whole idea of assembling masses of students (raw material) to be processed by teachers (workers) in a centrally located school (factory) was a stroke of industrial genius. The whole administrative hierarchy of education followed the model of industrial bureaucracy."

However, modern society has no use for this rigid form of learning. Toffler believed that "the technology of tomorrow requires not millions of lightly lettered men [and women], ready to work in unison at endlessly repetitive jobs, it requires not men who take orders in unblinking fashion . . . but men who can make critical judgments, who can weave their way through novel environments, and who are quick to spot new relationships in a rapidly changing reality."

So what should a modern approach to education look like? Toffler's vision was revolutionary. He argued that colleges should be more flexible and responsive to the needs of students. He believed that institutions should make room for more diverse students and older "lifelong" learners. They must encourage students to learn outside the classroom through internships and apprenticeships. Lectures and note-taking must be abandoned in favor of experiential learning and group projects.

Toffler was among those who predicted a highly complex, highly technological future. He imagined a world filled with powerful computers, portable communication devices, and a radical rearrangement of Western society and its values. In flights of fancy he assumed that humans would colonize space, and he was quite sure that even small children should be taught how to live in undersea colonies.

Yet, even as he spun tales of a twenty-first century that looked like a *Jetson's* cartoon, Toffler argued for an education that offered more than just technical training. He was arguing for some very traditional skills, such as writing, speaking, critical thinking, and research skills. "Tomorrow's schools must," he believed, "teach not merely data, but ways to manipulate it. [Students] must learn how to learn."

Practical Liberal Arts

Today, the traditional approach to college education is criticized not only by futurists but also by many educators who think that sitting in classrooms, taking multiple-choice tests, dividing knowledge into separate intellectual compartments, and training for one particular career are strategies of an antiquated society. The emerging strategy is to show how all knowledge is connected and to find ways to create greater student involvement in the learning process.

Toffler predicted what has come to be the near-unanimous assertion of college leaders around the country. In the modern world, skills—even whole professions—become obsolete nearly as fast as they are created. And the skills needed to get that first job are not necessarily the skills needed to advance in your career or adapt to future changes. President Kenny puts it bluntly: "You don't become CEO if all you know is accounting."

In this climate, a growing number of colleges are promoting an education built around what some call the "practical liberal arts." The goal is to provide all students, regardless of their major, a strong grounding in the knowledge and skills needed to understand modern society and adapt to social and economic changes. According to a report by the AAC&U, this new philosophy of education "depends less on a particular subject matter than on an approach to teaching and learning." The report continues: "A student can prepare for a profession in a 'liberal,' mind-expanding manner, or study the humanities or social sciences (traditional 'liberal arts' disciplines) narrowly and shallowly. Both small colleges and large universities can educate their students liberally, as can technical institutes."

This new philosophy of education differs from a traditional college education. The old approach—pioneered by Columbia University during World War I—was to teach the liberal arts through introductory or "survey" classes that were part of the general education curriculum. The goal was to add breadth to every student's undergraduate education by requiring enrollment in one or more courses in history, language, philosophy, and other liberal arts disciplines.

These courses are still a part of nearly every college curriculum, usually offered during the first year or two of study. Before concentrating on their majors, undergraduate students are expected to take a certain number of classes in these disciplines. As a result, in the first year of study a typical list of classes might include:

- *English Composition*
- *Introduction to Astronomy*

- *Spanish I*

- *History of the Renaissance*

Most students look forward to this part of their education, at least in theory. In a 2002 national survey of college freshmen, nearly two thirds said they wanted to "gain a general education and an appreciation of ideas." Unfortunately, this part of the curriculum often fails to live up to expectations. Confronted with a laundry list of introductory classes, many students begin to resent these required courses, which are viewed as barriers to their major and a burden they need to overcome.

Plainly stated, these introductory courses can be boring. For example, much of the information taught in freshman English or history often duplicates what is taught in many high schools. According to Kenny, "So much of general education is repetition of what [students] have done in high school, and that is a great crime. They study American History, *yet again*, or Western Civilization, *yet again*. The freshman year needs to be a time when [students] are really stimulated and excited about learning. The [curriculum] needs to be more expansive."

As a result, the liberal arts have acquired a dismal reputation and liberal arts colleges sometimes feel under attack. Liberal arts courses are looked upon as old, dusty, irrelevant, and a holdover from another era. Many students and faculty members have grown accustomed to separating the college curriculum into two distinct parts:

- *the so-called useful part (those classes that train students for work)*

- *the liberal arts*

This is a false division of knowledge, however. The liberal arts can be—and should be—just as meaningful and "useful" as any other part of the curriculum. Those things that are often emphasized in a strong liberal arts program are keys to success in any profession, and in life. Quality institutions know this and are finding ways to separate the liberal arts from its tweed-coat and dusty-chalk-board reputation and make it the center-piece of a twenty-first century curriculum. Literature, history, philosophy, and the arts are again being thought of as useful tools—ways to understand the world around us and the forces that shape modern society. In addition, when writing, speaking, and research are emphasized, students are given the most important skills needed for success—the ability to gather and communicate new information clearly and persuasively.

> *When writing, speaking, and research are emphasized, students are given the most important skills needed for success— the ability to gather and communicate new information clearly and persuasively.*

An integral part of this updated liberal arts education is not simply the kind of subjects taught, but *how* they are taught. A vital component of a liberal arts education is a curriculum that *requires* students to take an active role in

their education. In the classroom, this means opportunities to discuss and debate ideas with the professor. It means
working with other students on team projects. It means
breaking down barriers that separate faculty teaching and
research by working *with* professors on real research
projects. It also means extending learning beyond the classroom through participation in internships, service-learning
projects, or study-abroad programs.

Students as "Active Learners"

When students play a larger role in their own education they
are participating in what has become known as "active learning." An influential report by The Johnson Foundation
titled, *Seven Principles of Good Practice in Undergraduate
Education*, explained the philosophy this way:

> Learning is not a spectator sport. Students do not
> learn much just sitting in classes listening to teachers,
> memorizing prepackaged assignments, and spitting out
> answers. They must talk about what they are learning,
> write about it, relate to past experience, and apply it
> to their daily lives. They must make what they learn
> part of themselves.

Active learning helps students put theory into practice.
Students should not simply study management theory, they
should test it through an internship with a corporation. Students should not only learn about European history, they

should travel to where it took place. Loren Anderson argues that "this notion of learning is about as good as it gets." He goes on to say: "A key assumption is that the best kind of learning occurs when you learn in the classroom and develop hypotheses which you take out and test to see if they work. So if you're studying community organization and development in sociology you have a chance to get an internship in a community organization and see if the notions you are studying seem to apply and work. As a result, you modify your theory, bring it back to the classroom, study it, and talk about it."

This combination is the foundation for the best possible undergraduate education. Students learn not only facts; they learn the kinds of skills that are both flexible and durable. This is a richer and more exciting way to learn and it is also the most practical. The AAC&U believes that active learning "develops just those capacities needed by every thinking adult—analytical skills, effective communication, practical intelligence, ethical judgment, and social responsibility. In this way, it creates an educated citizenry and prepares students for good jobs and satisfying careers."

What Employers Want

For most students, college is all about getting ready for a specific career. A recent national survey of college freshmen found that more than 70 percent of the respondents said that "to get training for a specific career" was a very important reason for their decision to attend college. About the same percentage reported that "to be able to make more money" and "get a better job" were also very important reasons to enroll.

Especially in an uncertain economy, students want to arrive at a job interview with the right kind of resume— and the skills needed to get ahead. Yet many corporate leaders have long argued that graduates increasingly lack the basic skills

"Employers are looking for people with good writing and communication skills."

that are vital to success. In today's business environment, it is not enough to have a set of technical skills. Instead, recruiters are interested in hiring graduates with a broad range of skills, including the ability to write and speak clearly and persuasively, work as part of a team, and solve complex problems.

"I've had it demonstrated over and over again in my interactions with recruiters who come to campus," says A. Tariq Shakoor, director of career services at Emory University. "Employers are looking for people with good writing and communication skills. They're especially looking for people who have an appreciation and an understanding of diverse cultures. They're looking for people with foreign language skills, interpersonal skills, team skills, and research skills."

By the way of an example, he mentioned a visit to the campus by a large management firm. It wanted to hire a student for a prestigious internship position and actually chose a student majoring in the liberal arts over another candidate majoring in marketing. "So that's the final litmus test to the value of a liberal arts curriculum," says Shakoor, "because it's the recruiters who come to campus who set the parameters of what they are looking for in the ideal candidate."

Students and parents often think that the savvy approach to college is to specialize as soon as possible and not be distracted by the liberal arts "fluff." College administrators tell stories of parents who are upset with children who want to switch from a "practical" major, like business or finance, to an "unemployable" major, like English or philosophy—not realizing that business leaders are among the first to argue that the liberal arts play a vital role. "In periods of change, narrow specialization condemns us to inflexibility—precisely what we don't need," says David T. Kearns, former CEO of Xerox Corporation. "We need the flexible intellectual tools to be problem solvers and to be able to continue to learn over time."

Even when the economy is weak, the advantages of a liberal arts education will remain strong. In the information technology world, many employers actively seek out liberal arts graduates. Today's business leaders want employees who can think "outside the box." Companies are particularly interested in hiring liberal arts graduates for jobs that require good interpersonal skills.

In this setting, the future belongs to the liberal arts, argues business writer Roger Herman. "In the future, a classroom and experienced-based liberal arts education will be the core of the post-high school academic experience. All other learning will flow from this foundation. This doesn't mean all students should major in the liberal arts. But it does mean that all majors should incorporate the liberal arts."

A number of studies have shown that students who are educated in the liberal arts are, in fact, more employable and, more surprising perhaps, generally advance farther up the career ladder. According to *Guidance and Counseling*, a journal for career counselors, "As time passes, liberal arts graduates often reach career levels which equal or surpass those of their more specialized colleagues as upper levels of management seem to require the more general skills developed in a liberal arts program."

The Factory Model Resists Change

Today, many educators embrace the idea of nimble, flexible, and collaborative learning. A tour of Web sites and a casual review of viewbooks show students doing all the things Toffler and many educators had hoped for. Students are working in small groups, they're heading overseas, they're pursuing internships, and they're working side-by-side with faculty in research labs. All this suggests that the practical liberal arts curriculum is now the dominant form of learning in most colleges and universities.

However, appearances can be deceiving. While there is a great deal of support voiced for a liberal arts education, colleges and universities are often slow to change. The old factory model of learning remains stubbornly in place. Traditional methods of teaching—lectures, textbooks, and distribution requirements—remain dominant within many institutions. Educators like the idea of active learning but don't always put it into practice. "There is a disconnect between what universities say they are doing and what they are [really] doing," acknowledges Kenny.

This disconnect is caused by many forces. One is financial. It costs more to fully implement a practical liberal arts curriculum. Classes in which writing and speaking are emphasized, for example, work best when classes are small, which means more teachers and more classrooms are needed. Another relates to how colleges and universities are structured. The practical liberal arts requires faculty from different academic specialties to work together. It also means that colleges and universities must create a special place in the curriculum for a strong, integrated general education program; that is, colleges and universities must work outside of the traditional academic boxes.

On many campuses, these barriers are difficult to overcome. The good news is that more and more colleges and universities are revising their undergraduate programs in ways that genuinely reflect the richness of a liberal arts education and the philosophy of a quality college education. Finding institutions that make the practical liberal arts a priority is the focus of the next chapter.

chapter 4

the five criteria of a quality education

The last chapter described the kind of education that will best prepare students for life after college. It also hinted at some of the things students will do at these colleges. Now it's time to ask: "What does this kind of institution look like, and how can prospective students know that the colleges and universities they are considering actually make student-centered learning a priority?"

A Virtual College Tour

Most institutions now offer "virtual tours" on their Web sites. Visitors can click their way through the campus and see what the admissions office believes are the highlights of the institution. By the end of the tour, prospective students have at least a superficial understanding of what the campus looks like and what the institution can offer.

However, it is not always easy to separate institutions that are more student-centered and committed to a liberal arts education from those that are not. While virtual tours focus on buildings and programs, the practical liberal arts is a *philosophy* of education that is expressed through all that the college or university does. It shapes both what is taught and how it is taught. It influences how students interact with faculty and with each other. It determines what students choose to study. It even shapes how students spend their free time—both on and off campus.

If they look in the right place, parents and students can identify colleges and universities committed to this kind of learning. Innovative and student-centered institutions tend to provide a package of programs, courses, and services that reflect a genuine commitment to the kind of education that best prepares students for work and service in the twenty-first century. We posed the question, "What does a good college or university actually look like?" to a diverse assortment of presidents and educational leaders. We asked them to describe what students should look for when visiting campuses and reading the recruitment literature. Collectively, they describe five specific characteristics of quality:

1. A commitment to general education from the freshman year to the senior year

2. A commitment to writing, speaking, and critical-thinking skills for all students in all classes

3. A commitment to active learning

4. Opportunities to extend learning beyond the classroom

5. A diverse, intellectually active, and respectful community

Individually, each characteristic helps to create a stronger institution; collectively they accomplish even more. When all of the pieces are put together, they reflect a new approach to higher education, one that is uniquely tailored to the many needs of the college student of the twenty-first century. Using examples of excellence from different colleges and universities across the United States, it is possible to construct our own "virtual tour" of a quality college. By focusing on these five indicators of quality and asking some hard-hitting questions, it is possible to separate reality from public relations and find institutions that are worth considering.

1. A Commitment to General Education

When Shirley Ellis graduated from high school she went straight to work. For the next 15 years she supported herself and her young daughter as a waitress and bartender. But she hoped to get more from life. "I always wanted to go to college," she says, "but I never knew what to study." She briefly considered, then rejected, nursing. Years later Shirley finally found her true calling. "I was always good with my own finances. I purchased my own home. I was good with numbers at work. I thought accounting was what I should go into." With a clear goal in mind, she enrolled at St. Joseph's College in Rensselaer, Indiana. She kept waitressing but still managed to study full-time. Four years later she graduated with an accounting degree and is now employed by a nearby firm.

For sure, college is expensive and time-consuming. For many, it's a true hardship. So why bother? Shirley Ellis has a simple answer: a career. But even students who enroll right out of high school and are undecided about their major see higher education as, above all, a path to work. Indeed, many say they would skip college altogether if it didn't help them toward a career. After all, isn't that what college is all about? The answer is a qualified "yes," but there's more to the story. If college offered only training for a specific career, then Shirley would have taken nothing but accounting classes and gained little more than a set of technical skills.

Shirley wanted something else. Although she was motivated, first, by a desire to learn new job skills, she also expected higher education to give her more. "I was looking at getting polished and becoming well-rounded," she explains. She didn't know exactly what this meant, or how it would be accomplished. But she did believe that college would expose her to new ideas that would be valuable.

Education is viewed as a financial investment. Graduates are expected to earn back, with interest, all that they put in. But is that the only reason people go to college? Most prospective students say no. While employment may top their list of reasons, they hope college will offer other rewards.

Preparing for Life

Shirley Ellis, like most students, believes the opportunity for self-discovery and intellectual growth is also an important reason to attend college. According to data collected in 2002 by the Higher Education Research Institute at the University of California at Los Angeles, nearly 75 percent of surveyed students say learning about things that interest them is a priority. Fifty-nine percent believe the opportunity to "gain a general education and appreciation of ideas" should be part of the college experience. While most students feel the need to prepare for work, they also want to prepare for life.

While most students feel the need to prepare for work, they also want to prepare for life.

Research confirms that a college education can satisfy both. On average, college graduates are better prepared to enter the job market, but graduates are also better prepared to understand and contribute to society.

Picking a Major

Specialization comes through the major. When students "declare a major," it means they intend to focus on one particular subject area, and their choices are almost limitless. There are more than 6,000 distinct majors offered in America's colleges and universities, from engineering and education to Slavic languages and food service management. The popularity of these programs rises and falls over time, but career-oriented degrees now top the list.

In recent years, students have been more likely to choose a major that appears to make them more employable. The percentage of majors in business, engineering, health professions, and assorted technical fields, for example, has risen sharply. Meanwhile, the percentage of students majoring in English, history, art, and other liberal arts disciplines has dropped. For most students, the opportunity to specialize is the best part of college. At last, they have a chance to study what they want and prepare in a tangible way for their future. "What's your major?" is probably the most common question asked in college because it helps reveal something about the student and what he or she hopes to become.

But the major is only part of the college experience. Most students will complete about forty classes before they graduate, but in a typical program less than half of these classes are "in the major." What about the rest? The remainder of the program is filled up with electives—courses of the student's own choosing—and a set of classes collectively called general education.

A Place for General Education

General education introduces students to the breadth of the liberal arts. In contrast to the specialized and often technical training found in the most popular majors, general education is seen by many as an integral part of an undergraduate education.

However, a general education curriculum offers other, more practical rewards. In fact, some argue that skills learned as a natural part of a good general education program are the most enduring and most desirable to

> *General education introduces students to the breadth of the liberal arts.*

many employers. For example, those who can solve problems and adapt to new situations are the ones who are happiest and most successful in their careers.

At quality colleges and universities, general education is a true priority. Here, general education courses reveal how all knowledge is connected and relevant to students' lives. Students become more than "well-rounded." They leave with a new and deeper understanding of themselves and their place in the world.

Further, at these institutions, general education is more than just a few introductory courses in the arts, humanities and sciences. It's woven into the whole college experience. How can prospective students tell whether general education is a priority at the schools they are considering? Although 95 percent of American colleges and universities offer some form of general education, some make it an especially meaningful part of the curriculum. At these schools, students are carefully guided in their selection of general education classes and may complete a "core" of required classes.

Q & A

• *Does the college or university offer freshman-year seminars?* One of the best and most reliable ways to investigate a college or university's commitment to general education is to look at the courses all students are expected to take as soon as they arrive. Prospective students, especially, should find out if all or most students enroll in what are commonly called "freshman-year seminars" or "first-year programs." These seminars are academic courses that typically examine one topic—social, historical, or political—in depth and stress the use of college-level reading, writing, and researching skills.

The program at St. Lawrence University in Canton, New York, illustrates the richness of this approach to general education. Here, all incoming freshmen are immediately divided into fifteen "residential colleges" where they live and learn with approximately thirty other new students. Each of these mini-communities is taught by a team of two or three faculty members and lives in the same university dorm.

Every course in this first-year program explores a different theme. Recent topics of study ranged from

American history to Chinese medicine. One recent topic, taught by a team that included an economist and psychologist, was the examination of the family as an institution. Another, taught by a literature professor and a physicist, examined the literary genre of science fiction. In every case, a subject is explored in depth and from several different perspectives. What's more, learning is not confined to the classroom. Because students study and live together, the distinction between classroom study and the rest of college life is deliberately blurred. Learning happens around the clock, wherever students gather.

This program also helps set the tone for all four or more years of learning. Through class discussions, writing assignments, and library research, students build skills they will need throughout their college career—and in their lives after graduation. Living and learning with a small group of students with similar interests establishes an atmosphere of support. Camaraderie is built as students collaborate and commiserate. In this new environment, new students quickly become a part of the larger university community.

"This kind of program provides students with an integrated introduction to college," notes St. Lawrence's Associate Dean Steven Horowitz. "We have created a safety net. It's a support community for students making the transition to college both academically and socially. Rather than just throwing them out into four separate classes and then going back to a dorm where they might not know the person next door, this really roots them in a community."

The program at this one small university is part of a growing trend in higher education to focus more attention on the academic and social needs of first-year students. Too often, new students are abandoned after they arrive. While juniors, seniors, and graduate students enjoy smaller classes and more attention from faculty, new students frequently toil through large, often boring, introductory classes, succeeding or failing in relative anonymity.

> *New students need the most attention and deserve to take classes that are as creative and intellectually rich as the best graduate school seminars.*

This is no way to start a college career. New students need the most attention, not the least, and deserve to take classes that are as creative and intellectually rich as the best graduate school seminars. The new emphasis is on what some educators call "front loading." The support and personal attention once reserved for third- or fourth-year students is now available to first-year students. Creative interdisciplinary courses, taught even in the first semester, bring students into the college community and build academic skills.

Once considered novelties in higher education, these freshman-year programs, or first-year programs, are quickly becoming the norm. Both small liberal arts colleges and large research universities are offering and requiring these courses as a way of providing at least some exposure to the kind of active, interdisciplinary learning that is the hallmark of a quality education. A survey of research universities across the country found that 80 percent now offer some kind of academically oriented freshman-year seminar.

Freshman-year seminars fulfill many needs. They help students get oriented to college life and, because classes are usually small, communication skills are usually stressed. For these reasons, many educators consider these programs to be one of the most important trends in undergraduate education—the foundation of the entire undergraduate experience. This first year is a time when students should be treated as more than just a number. They should enroll in classes that satisfy their intellectual curiosity, and build research, writing, and critical-thinking skills that will help them during all four or more years of study and throughout their lives.

However, the quality of these programs varies. To get the full benefit of what these freshman-year programs provide, prospective students should look for colleges and universities that expect all students to complete one or more seminars. They need not combine living and learning. But like the program at St. Lawrence, they should focus on the study of an academic subject, be taught in small classes, and take advantage of all that this allows—active student participation, development of original research, and team projects.

They should also be taught by full-time faculty, not adjuncts or graduate students. Building meaningful relationships with full-time faculty is a vital part of what first-year programs are all about. A college or university that makes this commitment to its students during the first year of learning demonstrates an even deeper and richer commitment to a creative and coherent education during all four or more years of study.

• *Does general education extend from the freshman to the senior year?* Freshman-year seminars are a good start. But at a growing number of colleges, they are just one piece of a strong general education program. At the quality institutions, students are carefully guided through their selection of general education courses, through a core of required classes, and through a limited selection of optional courses created specifically for the general education curriculum. At these schools, general education is more than a random collection of courses that satisfy loose "distribution requirements." Rather, it is coherent, relevant, and interesting.

> *One of the strongest commitments to general education is found at institutions that go beyond distribution requirements and offer a "core curriculum."*

A quick examination of an institution's course catalog will help prospective students pick out the quality institutions. First, find out how many general education classes are offered, advises Arthur Levine, president of Teachers College at Columbia University. "Avoid any school that has a list of possible [general education] courses longer than your arm," he proposes. When students pick from a large menu of optional courses, cafeteria style, essential connections are too often lost.

Also look at the titles of general education classes. Do they appear to be connected to each other? Are they presented in a logical sequence? "If not, you can bet the requirements have not been carefully thought out," says Levine.

One of the strongest commitments to general education is found at institutions that go beyond distribution requirements and offer a "core curriculum." At these schools, all students take the same general education classes. Undergraduates complete as many as ten or more core classes, usually in the same order. Saint Joseph's College, for example, has a model core curriculum. In fact, the whole sequence of required general education classes is simply called "Core." Here, all students complete ten required courses, spread over all four or more years of study. Together, students and faculty examine, in a carefully organized sequence, history, science, philosophy, and different cultures. The curriculum stresses how each influences the other and how this knowledge can be applied to the student's major.

For example, "Core One," the first course taught in the freshman year, looks at modern American history. It meets five days a week—twice in a large hall where all freshmen gather for a formal lecture and three times in small discussion classes with just fifteen to eighteen other students. It is a 6-credit course—the equivalent of two regular classes—and fills nearly half of students' course schedules. "Core Two" is taken by freshmen during their second semester. It steps back in time and studies the seventeenth to the twentieth centuries, examining not just historical events but also the values of each era and how they were expressed.

During the sophomore year students study the Greeks and Romans, examining the roots of Western civilization. In the third year, students also take "Core Science," which examines the scientific method through reading, discussion, and hands-on work in the lab. They also study non-Western cultures. In their senior year, the core curriculum ends with an exploration of the Christian faith, encouraging students to think about their own beliefs.

While all this may seem daunting, many graduates believe it was the richest part of their college experience. "Alums will come back and talk about what they learned in core," says JaLeen Dearduff, a current St. Joseph student who also works in the academic affairs office. "You do see the value of it once you graduate and are out there in the real world."

A few other institutions have a similar program of study. Mount Saint Mary's College in Emmitsburg, Maryland, for example, offers a sequence of nineteen core courses spread over all four or more years of learning. Half of each student's course load is reserved for these classes. "All students take the same classes and basically in the same order," says Provost Carol L. Hinds.

These schools reflect different approaches to general education. Yet each represents a serious commitment to liberal learning. We encourage you to look for schools that follow one of these approaches, and pick the one that reflects your own needs and interests.

2. A Commitment to Writing, Speaking, and Critical-Thinking Skills

One of the clearest messages coming from both educators and employers is that success depends on good communication skills. Unfortunately, this is a skill too many college graduates fail to master. Employers loudly complain that even top students from competitive schools are frequently unable to write clearly or make persuasive presentations.

> *One of the clearest messages coming from both educators and employers is that success depends on good communication skills.*

Most students find themselves enrolled in at least one required English composition course. In most traditional "English comp" courses, students are asked to complete a few relatively short papers in proper research-paper format. Topic sentences, paragraphing, in-text citations, and other matters of proper form are addressed. Students complete the class and then move on to other courses in their own major, where they may—or may not—make use of these skills. Therein lies the problem.

In a traditional college curriculum, writing and presentation skills are not connected to the rest of the college experience. Students learn a few skills that often seem irrelevant to them because they are separated from real research and their own academic interests. ("English comp" can be painfully boring when in the hands of anything but the most enthusiastic and inspired professor.)

But institutions committed to quality education have a different perspective. They argue that writing is not just about grammar and literature. It's about *communication*. It's a tool used by all professions to explain necessary information and present new ideas. At these schools, the strategy is not to segregate communication in one or two composition courses but to make it

> *Communication is not just one more subject to study—like history or math—it is an integral part of the teaching and learning process of all disciplines.*

a part of the whole college experience. It is a skill continually used and refined by all students in all majors and during all four or more years of study. In other words, communication is not just one more subject to study—like history or math—it is an integral part of the teaching and learning process of all disciplines. And the benefits are felt long before graduation. When writing and speaking are built into the curriculum, students think more deeply about the subjects they study, making the whole college experience richer.

A student at the University of Missouri explains: "I learn more when I have to sit down and write a paper. I take time to think about it. In classes where we take tests, I just cram and forget most of what I learned."

When evaluating colleges and universities, look for those that do more than offer one or two required English courses. A quality institution makes reading, writing, and critical thinking part of each student's whole college experience. While this may sound intimidating, the rewards are real.

Q & A

• *Are English language skills formally taught during the freshman year?* Courses that focus on English language skills should be a part of every new student's class schedule. This is not a happy thought for some students. Many have lost all interest in English by the time they enter college, convinced that the emphasis will be on illogical grammar rules and tedious writing exercises. Instructors are aware of their reputations as nitpickers. "Our students, and much of the population, believe that the English teacher's job is to sniff out errors and to punish students for making them," acknowledges Laurence Musgrove, director of composition at the University of Southern Indiana in Evansville.

Students are also convinced by the time they enter college that writing is a talent possessed by only a fortunate few. It is not seen as a skill that can be taught or learned. Many feel that writers are born and not made."Our culture doesn't promote the idea that good writing is possible for everyone," Musgrove says. "They see it as something that newspaper people or people with a special gift do." But when taught well, these courses rebuild lost confidence and teach essential skills. At the introductory level, classes should emphasize the elements of clear and persuasive writing. They should develop research skills and help students learn how to analyze information in sophisticated ways.

Traditionally, these skills are developed in English composition courses taught by English faculty or writing instructors. At the University of Southern Indiana, for example, all new students enroll in "English 101," where writing and critical-thinking skills are nurtured. At the College of New England in Henniker, New Hampshire, freshmen complete a year-long "College Writing" course. In this class, students learn how to develop a research paper and follow accepted style rules. Similar courses are offered at institutions across the country.

Some institutions have done away with the traditional English composition course requirement and have chosen to develop writing and research skills during the first year of study through freshman seminars or similar interdisciplinary courses. This strategy makes the dreaded research paper more interesting and meaningful for students because, as Steven Horowitz observes, "Now [students] have a course where they are writing about *something*. You have a group of students taking the course because they've chosen to be there," he notes. "They have an intellectual interest in the subject. It's not just writing. It's speaking, it's research, and it's critical thinking. So it's an integrated approach to communication. It's *not* the five paragraph paper on what I did last summer."

Some freshman seminars place special emphasis on writing and speaking skills. At Bryn Mawr College in Bryn Mawr, Pennsylvania, students enrolled in a year-long course write a paper every week. They also meet individually with their professors every other week to discuss their writing. While the seminar is not a course in English, the emphasis on reading and writing is so strong that it satisfies Bryn Mawr's English composition requirement.

Gustavus Adolphus College in St. Peter, Minnesota, offers a first-term seminar created specifically to develop language skills. There, class sizes are small and each group of students investigates a different theme on subjects ranging from American history to computer science.

Whether taught formally through an English composition class or integrated into a freshman seminar, written and oral communication should be a priority during the first year of study.

• *Are writing and speaking required in every subject during all years of study?* To make sure students keep writing, many colleges and universities ask them to complete two or more writing-intensive courses during their four or more years of study. These are regular academic classes, taught by faculty within the different majors, that require students to complete a significant amount of writing.

Writing-intensive programs are now common at America's colleges and universities. At the University of Missouri–Columbia, for example, students begin writing during their first semester in a required English composition course. In order to graduate, they must also complete two writing-intensive courses—one in their major. Nearly seventy-five writing-intensive courses are offered at the university on subjects ranging from American art to invertebrate zoology.

The University of Wyoming in Laramie has nearly identical requirements, beginning with a freshman-year composition course, followed by two writing-intensive classes. The University of North Carolina at Greensboro also offers writing-intensive classes in all departments. Classes are small, allowing faculty members to work more closely with individual students. Many smaller institutions also feature writing-intensive courses.

These courses demonstrate a genuine commitment to language and critical thinking. But do they make a difference? Most instructors believe they do. "Students get better at expressing themselves," observes Aaron Krawitz, who is a material scientist teaching at the University of Missouri–

Columbia. "They learn to focus on the important issues, and they learn how to think about problems."

• *Is writing emphasized in every class?* At some colleges, every class becomes writing intensive. Eugene Lang College in New York City takes advantage of its size by keeping classes small and making writing and speaking a significant part of every class. Although two freshman-year writing seminars are required, the focus on language is pervasive. Classes at this college—which focuses on the social sciences and humanities—are limited to just fifteen students.

King College in Bristol, Tennessee, focuses on language through a curriculum that includes the study of classical and modern literature. Students write and discuss what they have read and even make creative use of the visual arts. First-year students, for example, may find themselves reading Homer or African-American author Zora Neale Hurston. They write essays, present speeches, and make group presentations. In the past, students also have rewritten and performed *Everyman*, a sixteenth-century morality play, using modern language and situations. Sophomores have presented mock news broadcasts from Camus's plague-stricken city of Oran, constructed board games based on Dante's *Inferno*, and evaluated the use of evidence in the movie *JFK*. In each of these programs, educators stress the practical value of their writing by emphasizing that if students can express themselves clearly and persuasively, they will be more successful in their chosen careers.

3. A Commitment to "Active Learning"

American colleges and universities have become experts in crowd control. A visit to any large institution during fall registration reveals how higher education is a learning industry. Students stand in lines, waiting for their turn with a registrar, cashier, adviser, or bookstore clerk. Progress is tracked, with mechanical precision, on computers. Social security numbers—not names or academic interests—are how students are identified.

Standing amid this organized chaos, it is easy to forget that learning is, above all, a human enterprise. Success is ultimately defined not by the efficient movement of bodies in and out of the institution. Instead, it is defined by the ability to reach out to all students and make them active partners in their own education.

Too often, the assembly line continues into the classroom. Large lecture halls define much of undergraduate education. In the largest classes, students may arrive and leave unknown to their professors.

Fortunately, there is evidence of change on campuses across the country. Colleges and universities are reorganizing their classrooms and, occasionally, their entire curricula to allow new styles of learning and to put the focus back on students. Faculty and administrators talk about "active learning"—the ability to engage students in their own learning.

At these institutions, students work closely with teachers and other students. Walk into a classroom and you will not see a formal lecture, but a conversation. Questions are

asked, answered, chal-
lenged, and respect-
fully discussed by all.
Students may even be
working in groups,
sharing ideas and re-

> *At quality institutions, active learning is supported across campus and students can step off the educational assembly line.*

sponsibility for assignments. Perhaps students have left the classroom; they might be found completing research in a laboratory, community, or even in another country.

At quality institutions, active learning is supported across campus and students can step off the educational assembly line. Each classroom becomes its own small, nurturing community where students have a voice and an opportunity to contribute.

Q & A

• *Do teachers know their students?* Active learning rarely takes place in a large lecture hall. Instead, an institution committed to more student participation must, as a first step, offer small classes and opportunities for out-of-class interaction with faculty. Here, students work closely with faculty. There is rapport between students and teachers, and the classroom becomes a true community. This is a fundamental first requirement for learning in the creative classroom, but it can only happen in small classes and small groups.

So when evaluating the quality of instruction, look first at the size of the classes. A college or university that values active learning offers more small classes, even in introductory freshman courses. When large lecture courses are necessary, they will be supplemented by small discussion groups.

Keep in mind that class size is a simple indicator of quality, but it is not always easy to evaluate. Recruitment literature from most colleges and universities—even the largest state institutions—often gives the impression that every student gets personal attention. If viewbooks reflected reality, then no class in American higher education would enroll more than a dozen students, and most classes would be held outside on warm spring days.

Most prospective students and their parents are justifiably skeptical of this literature. But they do pay attention to what appears to be a more reliable indicator: student-faculty ratios. The assumption is that institutions with a lower ratio offer smaller classes and can give more attention to each student.

But these numbers do not tell the whole story. A 12:1 ratio may sound good, but because this number is an average, it does not reveal the full range of class sizes. Although many juniors and seniors may enjoy small classes at this institution, required freshman and sophomore courses could still enroll hundreds of students.

Ratios are not enough to make an informed choice. When judging class sizes, investigate the institution more thoroughly. For example, find out not just the average class size but also the size of the largest classes taken by undergraduates. Most important, find out the size of the largest general education classes. These are the courses that are most often overloaded. The admissions office should have these figures if they are not reported in recruitment literature.

• *Do students participate in class?* It is not enough to know that a college or university offers small classes. Prospective students should also examine how classes are taught. Small classes are most important because they allow faculty members to teach in more flexible and innovative ways. With small classes and greater individual attention from teachers, students can contribute more in the classroom. There is no back row in these classes; faculty members encourage student participation and, in some cases, expect students to help direct the class.

How is this kind of participation encouraged? First, classes are taught as seminars, where students actively discuss and debate issues. In these courses, faculty members do not lecture; they guide discussions and encourage all students to participate. The teacher leads by posing questions and highlighting key points; the class has the energy and informality of a conversation.

All colleges and universities offer at least some seminar-style classes, but at quality institutions, this kind of learning is available to all students, during all four or more years of study. At Coker College in Hartsville, South Carolina, for example, nearly all courses are taught as seminars during all four or more years of study. No class has more than twenty students, and students and teachers sit together at specially designed roundtables to encourage conversation. Only science classes that include laboratory work are taught in classrooms with traditional desks and tables.

"The roundtable approach is active learning that involves the whole class as a team," says Frank Bush, executive vice president of Coker College. "Students not only learn their subject matter, they also learn how to think critically and

> *When students are expected to contribute in each class, they soon become confident and articulate learners.*

creatively and to express themselves in front of others." Bush says new students may be intimidated by this unusual classroom arrangement—there is no place to hide when sitting at a roundtable. But students quickly discover its benefits. When students are expected to contribute in each class, they soon become confident and articulate learners. "The change we see in our students from their freshman year to their senior year is unbelievable," he says.

When visiting campuses, prospective students should take advantage of opportunities to attend classes and examine how they are taught.

Do students contribute to the content of each class?

Do they interact with each other, or just with the instructors?

Do faculty members generate lively conversations that include most students?

Do students come to class prepared for discussion?

Is the mood of each class civil and respectful?

When touring the campus, you should also take note of how desks are arranged in the classrooms. Rows of desks facing a podium suggest that classes rely on faculty lectures. If the desks are bolted to the floor, then any other kind of learning becomes almost impossible. But if chairs are arranged less formally—in a circle or semicircle—then student participation is more likely.

• Do students spend time with faculty outside the classroom? Colleges and universities of all sizes recognize the importance of out-of-class interaction with teachers. Time spent talking in the office, home, or dormitory is often the most meaningful for students. Some of the most important opportunities for intellectual growth exist between classes, when students can engage their teacher on a one-on-one basis. These meetings can turn faculty members into mentors and friends. This happens naturally at many institutions. However, be sure to ask if the college or university you are considering encourages interaction between students and faculty.

Some institutions have adopted a unique calendar where students take just one course at a time. Colorado College in Colorado Springs has divided its academic year into eight three-and-a-half week segments, with each block devoted to a single class. Since students and professors are not distracted by other obligations, they can devote their full attention to the class and to each other. Professors have even held classes off campus for a day or even an entire month.

- **Do most students participate in faculty research?** The opportunity for discussion is the first benefit of small classes. But some colleges and universities also ask their students to learn in other ways. Students may also collaborate on assignments and special projects, sharing ideas and responsibility for the final product. One of the most helpful indicators of active learning outside the classroom is found at colleges and universities that encourage joint faculty-student research.

> *One of the most exciting movements in higher education is to bring students into the community of scholars and to make them partners in the research process.*

At most universities and many colleges, research is a major part of faculty work. Professors spend many hours in laboratories and libraries, completing scholarship for publication or presentations for professional conferences. In the past, most of this work was off limits to undergraduates who were thought to be too inexperienced to complete their own original research or assist faculty. Recently, though, many educators have had a change of heart.

One of the most exciting movements in higher education is to bring students into the community of scholars and to make them partners in the research process. Increasingly, they are completing their own research, presenting papers at professional conferences, and working side-by-side with scientists.

The movement to include students was championed by the nation's research universities. The goal was to turn a central mission of the university—scholarship—into an asset for undergraduates. Instead of making students the perpetual losers in the teaching versus research debate, the idea was to bring the two sides together and make research a function of teaching. A better win-win solution has never been devised in modern higher education.

This approach offered so many benefits to undergraduates that the movement has spread throughout higher education. Today, even small liberal arts colleges, which have traditionally promoted teaching over research, are encouraging student-faculty research on their campuses. Arthur Rothkopf, president of Lafayette College, considers opportunities for undergraduate research to be a key indicator of quality because it reveals so much about an institution's commitment to teaching, active learning, and the practical liberal arts in general. "Through research, students have an opportunity to explore their academic interests. They work closely with faculty. They have an opportunity to write and to publish. A lot of the research is then published as joint student-faculty publications," he says. "More important," he notes, "students are becoming the graduate assistants you would find at a research university. And whether they continue their education or not, it [the experience] is enormously valuable. We find it is one of the most important things we do."

Colleges and universities across the country are making undergraduates their research partners. At Spelman College, a historically black college for women in Atlanta, Georgia, most students take part in some kind of original research before graduation. They may help to conduct laboratory experiments or assist faculty members with their research. To broaden their experiences, students are encouraged to obtain internships during the summer at research universities across the country.

At Spelman, all students in the sciences take part in research and, overall, 60 percent of the entire student body leaves with experience in original research. Unfortunately, not all colleges and universities offer these kinds of opportunities. While student-faculty research is a hot trend, most colleges and universities fail to serve all, or even most, of their students.

A Healthy Balance

Before moving on, it's important to offer some kind words for the much-maligned lecture hall. Most students attend mid- to large-size universities; most of these schools offer lecture classes, many filled with hundreds of students. Is this bad?

Clearly, many believe education is made richer when students work with faculty members and with each other. This kind of learning should be available to all students, even freshmen, at all institutions. But, there is also a place for large-scale learning. For example, convocations may bring a department or an entire school together into an auditorium, helping to build a stronger sense of community and common purpose. In addition, some classes fill large lecture halls because student demand is so great. For example, Vincent Scully, a professor at Yale University, has delivered lectures for thirty years that attract 500 or more students at a time. Although his subject happens to be architecture, his skill and insight draw students from all disciplines. Many say his classes were the most memorable part of their education.

So we are not proposing that you avoid lectures at all costs (which would be impossible at most institutions). Rather, look for a healthy balance. The creative classroom comes in many shapes and sizes.

4. Opportunities to Extend Learning Beyond the Classroom

There is the odd belief that "learning" takes place only in classrooms under the direct supervision of professors. Equally odd is the established tradition of equating "knowledge" only with information contained in books and a few scholarly journals. Yet, that has been the guiding philosophy of higher education for years. Generations of students went to college where the world around them retreated into the background and the primary goal was to sit in enough classes and generate enough credits to graduate.

Quality institutions take a different approach to learning. While there is plenty to learn from books and in classrooms, these institutions know that an education is strengthened when learning is extended beyond the campus through work, internships, service projects, and overseas travel. These programs are another key indicator of a college or university's commitment to quality; students have an opportunity to practice what they have learned in the classroom and to learn in ways that no lecture can provide.

Just about every college and university allows students to participate in off-campus study and travel programs. In fact, many institutions actively encourage this kind of learning, and a growing number of institutions try to provide these experiences for most students.

Q & A

• *Do most students learn beyond the classroom?* At many colleges and universities, the boundaries between the classroom and community are falling away. They now encourage, and sometimes even require, students to earn credit for work and travel off campus. These experiences, when carefully organized and supervised by faculty, can be the most meaningful part of a student's education. They allow students to discover knowledge and apply what they have learned in ways that cannot be duplicated in any traditional classroom. It is the ultimate form of active learning.

Elon University in Elon, North Carolina, reports that it recently redesigned its curriculum and revamped more than 700 courses to put greater emphasis on learning beyond the classroom. All students are now required to take part in fieldwork by completing internships or studying abroad. Also, many classes now take students out into the community where they become advocates for social and environmental reform.

For example, one class studied the region's social needs, and another helped save a family homestead from being turned into a landfill. A philosophy course also requires students to complete a service project to show that "philosophy is not just a mind game," says Clair Myers, dean of arts and sciences. Some students have met this requirement by working with residents at a convalescent home.

When looking at colleges and universities, find out if opportunities for off-campus learning exist. Also ask how

students are helped to make these experiences a meaningful part of their academic studies.

How are they guided and advised during their work?

*How are they expected to transfer the knowledge they
gained back into the classroom?*

The goal is not simply to send students away, but to
encourage students to integrate what they learn off campus with what they study in the classroom.

At Queens University of Charlotte in North Carolina,
for example, *all* students complete internships, and more
than 90 percent take part in an overseas program. Both are
integral parts of the curriculum. In the internship program,
students prepare by completing an introductory course
called, "The World of Work." Next come two semester-long
internships, usually during the junior year. Internships
complement the interests of students—some head off to
corporate offices, while others work with nonprofit social
service agencies. In every case, students earn academic credit
and learn by sharing their experiences through reflective
journals and weekly class meetings.

The international travel program is equally well integrated into the curriculum. Again, travel is preceded by a
semester-long course that combines the study of history,
geography, politics, and the language and culture of the
country or region to be visited. On site, history majors can
see where an event took place, while environmental studies

majors can dive below oceans and climb mountains. Because this program is an integral part of the curriculum, the cost of the experience is built into the tuition and academic credit is provided.

• *Is service learning part of the curriculum?* Education is not simply a path to personal opportunity. Rather, it is a tool for social renewal. Knowledge and skills learned in college should help build a stronger nation. Every institution should encourage this kind of contribution, and a growing number do. Many incorporate service learning into specific courses, while others sponsor offices that help place students into the community. At some schools, this work is voluntary; at others it is required for graduation.

What kind of work do students complete? At Santa Clara University in Santa Clara, California, students work in a homeless shelter, a senior center, and help teach English as a second language to adult students. Calvin College in Grand Rapids, Michigan, has a service-learning center that places students in day-care centers, food banks, and environmental organizations. Many campuses also work with Habitat for Humanity, a nonprofit organization that helps build low-cost housing.

The list is almost endless, reflecting the needs of each community. But in each case, these programs show that individuals can make a difference, and students often say that they were the ones who gained the most.

At a minimum, a college or university should provide a clearinghouse for students looking for service-learning opportunities. Ideally, this will be a requirement for graduation and formally incorporated into the curriculum.

The practical value of all these programs is confirmed by A. Tariq Shakoor at Emory University, where more than 75 percent of students participate in some kind of internship or volunteer experience.

> *"Part of our encouragement is to wake up the kids and ask them to take charge of their own learning."*

"What makes us feel good about this is that companies and corporations also have a high regard for people who are involved in community service. Graduate schools look favorably on students who have had a well-rounded college experience that includes internships, volunteer experience, and study abroad."

But these programs do more than prepare students for employment. They broaden awareness of other cultures and other ideas. This is an equally important part of a quality education. "We have a generation of students who are attacking college as the next stage in what they are *supposed* to do," argues Butler University President Bobby Fong, "Part of our encouragement is to wake up the kids and ask them to take charge of their own learning. We encourage students to study abroad and to participate in internships and service learning."

Like these rich programs, quality institutions not only offer opportunities for work and study off campus but also make them an integral part of every student's education. Most students find that these experiences become the most memorable and most important part of their college career.

5. A Diverse, Intellectually Active, and Respectful Community

College is more than just classes. After all, even a full-time college student may spend only a few hours a day in the classroom. Colleges and universities are also communities— places where students work, make friends, and live. Quality institutions understand that the time spent out of class is just as important as the time spent in class and work to ensure that all students are treated with respect.

At these institutions, students may use their free time to attend a lecture by a Nobel laureate, participate in a student-produced play, chat with faculty in a residence hall lounge, participate in intramural sports, or write for the school newspaper. Leadership skills are nurtured within student government and in student organizations across campus. There also are special programs for commuter students and nontraditional learners.

Finding an institution that feels like a warm and welcoming community is an individual process—part of evaluating a

Finding an institution that feels like a warm and welcoming community is an individual process—part of evaluating a school's "fit."

school's "fit." Students who are happy at one institution may feel out of place at another. But even as students wander through campus, talk with students, and think about how comfortable the campus feels, it is worthwhile to examine four specific indicators of a strong campus community.

Q & A

• *Is the college or university a safe community?* Prospective students should evaluate the most fundamental requirement of a good community—the incidence of crime. For more than a decade, all colleges and universities have been required by federal law to collect and report the number and variety of crimes committed on their campuses. It's often difficult to compare institutions—a large urban campus may work harder to ensure safety but still have more crime than a small rural college. That said, prospective students have a right to know the incidence of theft and physical attacks in the past year and to know how the institution promotes student safety.

Many colleges and universities are working harder to guard personal safety. Police escort services, for example, are now common on many campuses; campus police or volunteers are available to accompany students who must walk across campus at night. Many schools have increased security in residence halls and other buildings. When visiting campuses, prospective students should ask students how safe they feel and how well the institution responds to victims of crime.

• *Is the college or university a respectful community?* Students should examine not just the level of crime but also the level of respect and trust shown among students. An institution is a healthy community only when all of its members treat each other with respect. Many colleges and universities have codes of conduct that guide academic behavior; some institutions make these honor codes an especially meaningful part of campus life. At these institutions, students understand the standards for behavior and abide by these rules. Infractions are treated with fairness and consistency.

At Harvey Mudd College, part of the Claremont Colleges in southern California, the honor code was established by and run by students. It applies to all academic matters and to the safety of private and public property. Infractions are heard by student-run judiciary and disciplinary boards. Adherence to the honor code creates more than a safe community. It allows students to learn in more flexible ways and to take full advantage of campus resources at any hour of the day. Students have 24-hour access to academic buildings, research labs, and computer equipment without supervision. Professors give timed, closed-book take-home exams. They also allow students to collaborate on assignments.

Other colleges have built an atmosphere of trust in similar ways. Rhodes College in Memphis, Tennessee, has a student-governed honor system that administrators and students say is respected. How do they know? "I've seen people fail a take-home test," explained one student. "That says to me that something is working." When looking at colleges and universities, make sure a clear code of student conduct exists and look for evidence that it is taken seriously by staff, faculty, and students.

Campus safety requires more than lights and locks. In the end, it depends on an atmosphere of respect, concern for others, and trust. "Campuses sometimes make a mistake by responding to just one issue, like sexual abuse," says Jim Carr, executive vice president at Harding University in Searcy, Arkansas. "But if students were taught respect for others, it would solve so many other problems."

• *Is the college or university a creative, intellectually engaged community?* Be sure to look for evidence that a significant percentage of students are active in the extracurricular life of the college or university. Participation in student government, clubs, and other organizations helps build a more interesting community and demonstrates that students are socially engaged and intellectually curious. It might indicate that the institution also takes extracurricular life seriously and provides

> *A campus that represents the nation's ethnic and racial diversity is not only showing an important commitment to educational equity but also that it is working hard to build a more diverse climate for learning.*

real opportunities for student leadership. At some colleges and universities, for example, student government representatives also vote for the college's board of trustees.

At the same time, it is important to look critically at the influence of sororities and fraternities. They play an important role in many college and university communities; they build camaraderie among members and sponsor community service projects. Yet, on too many campuses, they almost completely define student social life and tend to divide, not unify the campus. Blatant acts of racism, sexism, and brutality during initiation hazings have tarnished the image of some. Prospective students should find out if any have been cited for violations of alcohol policies and also the degree to which they set the tone for the college or university's social life.

• *Does the college or university promote diversity?* Students should pay close attention to evidence of diversity on campus. A campus that represents the nation's ethnic and racial diversity is not only showing an important commitment to educational equity but also that it is working hard to build a more diverse climate for learning. Preparing for life after graduation includes learning how to work with people of different backgrounds and points of view. Many educators believe that one of the most important benefits of a college experience is the opportunity to broaden horizons. The percentage of students who represent different groups—as well as other nationalities—may indicate that the institution is responding to the realties of the twenty-first century.

This vision of diversity is embraced at Bloomfield College in Bloomfield, New Jersey, where 48 percent of the students are African American, 17 percent are Hispanic, and 4 percent are Asian. Only one third are white. This mix did not happen accidentally. The college was started as a Presbyterian seminary for German immigrants in the last century, many of whom arrived at nearby Ellis Island. But the surrounding community changed, new immigrants arrived, and the college changed.

College officials do more than simply recruit minority students, however. They have made diversity the centerpiece of the college's mission. "A conscious effort was made not just to change with the changing demographics, but to dedicate ourselves to the population we serve," says Lourdes Delgado, dean of admissions. The college deliberately works to increase the number of minority faculty. Twenty percent of the teachers are African American, for example. In addition, the curriculum tries to reflect different cultures and acknowledge different traditions. "All courses, including the physical sciences, are required to approach their disciplines from a multiracial and multicultural perspective," says Delgado.

This philosophy prepares students of all races for the future. "The reality of our society is that it is no longer a largely white community. We're preparing kids for the kind of world we live in," she says.

Most colleges and universities are less heterogeneous. But diversity should be the goal of every institution. When examining an institution, look for a commitment to minority students and, of special importance, find out how the curriculum and faculty reflect changes taking place in America.

Diversity also requires an international perspective. Quality institutions enroll students from around the world and reflect global concerns in the curriculum through guest lectures, cultural presentations, festivals, and more. America is the favorite destination for international students. However, foreign students too often have little impact on most campuses. While a college or university will boast that it attracts learners from many countries, these students are usually not asked to contribute to the rest of the college community. At most institutions, they are a small, voiceless minority.

A commitment to international understanding requires more than the presence of international students. These students should be encouraged to participate fully in campus activities. Find out not only the percentage of international students but also investigate what role they play on campus.

Assessing Your Virtual Tour

Each of these five indicators of quality offers students a richer, more creative, and more relevant education. But the real value is found when all the pieces are put together. A college or university that works diligently to serve under-graduate students in all five areas is doing more than just pushing bodies through a credentialing assembly line. It un-derstands what it means to be truly educated and what stu-dents need to succeed, not only in their first job but throughout their lives.

By exploring each of the five indicators of quality and asking the fifteen questions posed in this chapter, it is pos-sible to confidently assess any institution's commitment to education. Assessments of quality need not be left to ex-perts and rankings. Quality is accessible to all.

chapter 5
measuring a quality education

With the escalating cost of higher education, many families are asking whether college is worth the investment. Although educators say yes, parents and students want proof. More than ever, Americans are asking how higher education makes a difference.

The focus is on what educators call the "outcomes" of higher education. It is no longer enough to say students are educated—and better prepared for life—just because they went to college. Instead, colleges and universities now examine what all students learn and track their progress after they leave. In some cases, students are asked to complete standardized tests, compile portfolios of their work, or respond to surveys.

Assessment is also an opportunity for students. It should be a time for "self-examination"—an opportunity to reflect on all they have learned, see how the parts fit together, and prepare for life after college.

Putting the Pieces Together

Between the first and last day of college, most students have spent at least four years on campus. They have completed dozens of courses, countless tests, research papers, and oral reports. Ideally, many have studied overseas or completed an internship; some have done both. All requirements have been met and a diploma is due, but before students don cap and gown, one final question must be asked: What have they learned?

> *In the end, all students should leave with not only the skills needed to earn a living but also the insight required to solve problems, to make wise decisions, and to advance the common good.*

This question is difficult to answer. Of course, it is possible to describe the individual pieces of a college education (students can list the classes they have taken and some of the facts they have learned). But it is much harder to put the many pieces together and examine the meaning and impact of the whole college experience.

Fitting the pieces together goes to the heart of a quality education. In the end, all students should leave with not only the skills needed to earn a living but also the insight required to solve problems, to make wise decisions, and to advance the common good. Ultimately, knowledge gained in the classroom and across campus must guide students throughout a lifetime—as both workers and citizens. If this higher purpose is not achieved, then students have ultimately gained little more than a sack full of academic credits.

Aware of this, today's quality colleges and universities ask students to reflect on how the many pieces of their education add up to a coherent whole. In their final months of study, for example, seniors may complete a comprehensive paper or take part in a senior seminar where social and ethical issues are discussed—in light of insights gleaned from all their classes and extracurricular experiences. Many schools track student progress after graduation: Alumni surveys find out if former students are satisfied with their careers and have benefited in other important, if less tangible, ways. These insights help schools refine the curriculum, services, and even their mission. In this way, students become partners in education reform.

> *More than anything else, undergraduate education is about the search for connections—within the curriculum and to the world beyond.*

More than anything else, undergraduate education is about the search for connections—within the curriculum and to the world beyond. The whole college experience, at its best, is a seamless web, with each part supporting the other. But how are these parts brought together, and how do students show they understand and apply to their own lives the larger goals of higher education?

The Big Picture: Senior Seminars

In senior seminars—also called "capstone" courses—students typically explore significant social or political issues in their last year of study, applying what they have learned to larger problems.

The University of Wisconsin–Green Bay offers a variety of senior seminars, each organized around a significant intellectual or social problem. All are taught as small discussion and writing-intensive classes and include students from a wide range of majors. According to Irene Kiefer, executive director of university communication, this allows students to "extend, apply, and integrate knowledge." For example, "The science student will bring a totally different perspective than someone who has been in the business program. Faculty members work hard to include these different views," she says.

At many colleges, the senior seminar is a time for students to apply what they have learned to real-life ethical and moral issues. Management students, for example, might talk about business ethics. They use writing and critical-thinking skills first introduced in freshman English classes as they research and defend their positions. They may refer to information taught in courses ranging from philosophy to science and think about the practical lessons they learned through internships and off-campus study.

Ideally, the colleges and universities that you are considering make senior seminars a required part of each student's education. Students should be expected to demonstrate their ability to write clearly and apply theoretical knowledge to practical problems.

A Bridge to Work: Senior Projects

The senior project is the culmination of college learning—the undergraduate equivalent of a master's thesis. In fact, at many colleges and universities, it is called the senior thesis and is expected to be a piece of original research.

At other colleges and universities, the senior project can take many different shapes. For example, it may be a dance performance, art exhibit, or detailed business plan, depending on the student's major. In many cases, these projects help students make the transition into their first career. In essence, the senior project is a bridge to the real world. For example, one management student met the requirement by studying how to start an art supply business. A

Vietnamese student learned how to market insurance to the Vietnamese community in Boston. There are other examples of students who presented their senior projects to potential employers as a tangible demonstration of their ability.

At most schools, the final requirement is a public presentation of the project. Students have a prescribed amount of time to talk about their findings and respond to questions from faculty, outside evaluators, students, and other members of the college community. The senior project is an important part of a quality institution's core curriculum and plays a part in the assessment process. By completing independent research or a creative project, students are demonstrating the full breadth of their knowledge. This helps educators serve students even better. At the University of South Carolina at Aiken, new courses have been added and existing courses changed after faculty members identified weaknesses in the senior projects completed by their students. This kind of formal institutional assessment is another way colleges and universities are becoming more accountable.

Impact of Student Outcomes

All colleges and universities want their graduates to be successful. A school's credibility grows when its students find good jobs or are admitted to prestigious graduate schools. Many colleges and universities now track student progress after graduation, eager to learn how they are doing. They survey graduates to find out how many are employed, how much they earn, and how many go back to school to further their education.

Many colleges and universities use these data when recruiting new students. Johnson & Wales University in Providence, Rhode Island, which offers degrees in food service and hospitality at five campuses across the country, reports that more than 95 percent of its graduates find jobs within sixty days. Kalamazoo College in Kalamazoo, Michigan, states that between 85 and 95 percent of its graduates who applied to law and medical school in recent years were admitted. Fort Lewis College in Durango, Colorado, found that more than 50 percent of alumni describe their job level as "professional" or "upper management." The message to potential students: "Our graduates are successful—you will be too!"

This kind of tracking serves two purposes. It highlights strengths and uncovers weaknesses and leads to improvement. In this way, student outcomes become an important part of the assessment process and ultimately create an even stronger institution. When considering a college or university, do some research to determine whether:

- *All graduates complete formal surveys that ask questions about all aspects of their college experience*

- *Surveys are completed soon after graduation*

- *Follow-up surveys are completed in later years, and how the results of those surveys are used*

- *Changes have been made to the curriculum, campus activities, or student services in response to survey results*

Earlham College in Richmond, Indiana, sends out surveys one, five, and ten years after graduation. The one-year survey asks students if their undergraduate education helped them in their work or graduate program. Later surveys ask students to reflect more deeply on their experiences in college and the values they taught:

- *How do they feel about their major, the financial aid office, the social life?*

- *Do they feel the college prepared them professionally?*

- *Are they actively involved in political and social issues?*

These and dozens of additional questions search for meaningful insights about the institution and its lasting influence on those who attend it.

What has Earlham College found in its survey results? Graduates said good things about the college, but there was room for improvement. For example, the career services office received relatively low marks from students responding to recent five- and ten-year surveys. "I could have used some exposure to internships and practicums," one student wrote.

"But I, like a lot of students, was too lazy to find the career center and pursue this on my own." In response, Wendy Seligmann, director of the career development center, took action. She now makes presentations to classes, telling students about her office and especially about the value of internships. In one recent class, all students were required to identify ten internships—and actually apply to one. This is just one example of how student surveys can make a lasting impact on schools.

Of course, these surveys also provide insight for prospective students. In addition to the pieces of data featured in viewbooks, an institution should be willing to share the full findings of its research. Seligmann says that survey data are available to all prospective Earlham College students through her office.

Other colleges and universities collect similar data in other ways. Some conduct formal exit interviews, examine portfolios of student work, and even interview employers. In each, educators gain a better understanding of the needs of students, the impact of

However, at its best, assessment focuses on the larger goals of higher education, not just data about student employment, income, or graduate study.

higher education, and the strengths of their institutions. However, at its best, assessment focuses on the larger goals of higher education, not just data about student employment, income, or graduate study.

Ready for the Future

When they graduate, students leave college with a credential and skills that prepare them for a career or further study.
When they graduate from a *quality* college, they have gained
even more.

**1. Students leave with a mastery of the English lan-
guage.** Freshman seminars, writing-intensive classes, and senior research have built proficiency in the most essential of

all human skills. More
than minimally com-
petent, students have
learned to make lan-
guage a powerful tool.
In addition, through a
core curriculum and

*A campus that reflects—and
celebrates—America's rich ethnic diversity prepares students
for changes taking place in the
nation.*

enriched major, students leave with essential skills, as well
as an ability to find connections across the disciplines and
to life beyond campus. From the freshman through the
senior year, students are guided through a logical sequence
of courses that add up to a coherent whole.

**2. Students have learned to take charge of their own
education.** They are active participants in classroom discussions and collaborate with other students and faculty
members on common projects. They may have created independent study projects and participated in research and
now can find and apply information contained in books,

periodicals, and computers. The skills and confidence taught in college help them make the transition to work with greater ease and prepare them for a lifetime of learning.

3. Students are ready to contribute to society. A focus on service reminds students that we all have a responsibility to build strong, caring communities. Leadership skills are nurtured through student government and student organizations.

4. Students are prepared to join a diverse workforce. A campus that reflects—and celebrates—America's rich ethnic diversity prepares students for changes taking place in the nation.

chapter 6
the end of rankings?

For American higher education, these are boom times. College enrollments continue to grow and the percentage of Americans who have earned a college degree climbs with each generation. Today, the majority of high school graduates choose to continue their education. If higher education is likened to any other consumable good—like cars, jeans, or fast food—it would be a very hot product, indeed.

But not all is well in the world of higher education. Rapid growth, spiraling tuition, and increased campus diversity force educators to confront such difficult and uncomfortable questions as:

- *How should colleges and universities serve all who want to buy their product?*

- *What does quality mean at a time when higher education must be manufactured with the speed and efficiency of a McDonald's hamburger?*

- *What is the value of education when diplomas are as ubiquitous as Big Mac wrappers?*

For most of America's history, colleges and universities were on the defensive. They were viewed as havens for dandies who learned esoteric facts and were out of touch with the "real world." Nearly 300 years ago, a young Benjamin Franklin (who never went to college) mocked the pretensions of Harvard students who, as he said, "learn little more than how to carry themselves handsomely and enter a room genteelly," graduating "as great blockheads as ever, only more proud and conceited."

As recently as the 1970s, a few scholars were still arguing that college was not the only way or even the best way for Americans to gain knowledge or prepare for a career. Assuming that higher education was the right choice for all young people made colleges a dumping ground for millions of uninspired youth who had nothing better to do. Carolyn Bird, author of *The Case Against College*, put it best when she wrote, "The great majority of our nine million postsecondary students who are 'in college' are there because it has become the thing to do or because it is a pleasant place to be."

Like several other critics, Bird argued that colleges and universities engaged in a kind of fraud by flooding the nation with more graduates than it could gainfully employ. There was simply no way that the thousands of students majoring in psychology, anthropology, creative writing, and dozens of other specialties were all going to find work related to their discipline. "A lot of jobs that attract the liberally educated come under the heading of nice work for the few who can get it," she wrote.

These arguments are rarely heard today. While it is true that students majoring in traditional liberal arts subjects may not find work directly related to their discipline, the advantage of a college degree makes most criticism of this sort look picky and irrelevant. The bottom line is that those who complete college are not only more likely to be employed, they will

The bottom line is that those who complete college are not only more likely to be employed, they will probably earn more— a lot more—than those who do not go to college.

probably earn more—a lot more—than those who do not go to college. According to the American Council on Education, "The annual differential between the salary of high school graduates and bachelor's degree recipients grew from $13,667 per year in 1998 to $20,630 in 1999."

Colleges and universities are riding a crest of public approval. While critics such as Carolyn Bird viewed colleges as "youth ghettos" and even prisons, most Americans now see them as facilitators of opportunity. A recent survey sponsored by the *Chronicle of Higher Education* found that most people—even those without a college degree—are cheerleaders for higher education. "At a time when Americans are anxious about the direction in which the country is headed, when they widely mistrust corporations, and express little confidence in their public schools, their faith in American higher education remains at extraordinary levels," the *Chronicle* summarized. More than 90 percent of respondents either agreed or strongly agreed that colleges and universities are one of the most valuable resources in America.

An Essential Good?

But there is more to the story. Colleges and universities provide a strong economic advantage, not just because they provide skills and knowledge but also because they have *replaced* nearly all other paths to a career. Not long ago, it was possible to find opportunities for both entry-level work and career advancement without a degree—from copy boy to city editor, from draftsman to architect, from stockroom to boardroom. This clearly is no longer the case. Except in certain trades, the college degree has replaced apprentice-

> *Colleges and universities provide a strong economic advantage, not just because they provide skills and knowledge but also because they have* replaced *nearly all other paths to a career.*

ships and the school of hard knocks. Indeed, even the bachelor's degree is no longer enough in many cases.

For those who want to advance in their careers, college is now a gate though which most Americans *must* pass. It is no longer one of the possible paths to opportunity, but the only path. "There are fewer ways to develop marketable skills and talents than there were a decade ago," acknowledges the American Council on Education. "The 'you can succeed without college' stories still appear in newspapers, but now they are couched as exceptions and are not put forward as a reasonable alternative for families to consider." College is not merely a good, but an "essential good."

Unfortunately, educators and the public have been slow to respond to the full implications of these changes. On the one hand, the nation embraces the values of inclusion and preaches that education is good for all. On the other hand, educators and the public too often cling to the fantasies of elitism. We still view college as an institution of prestige rather than an institution of access and opportunity. Colleges and universities are encouraged to focus on superficial indicators of quality—reputation and selectivity—and emphasize the value of the degree rather than the value of the educational experience.

The result is institutional confusion and a growing gap between the rhetoric and reality of undergraduate education. In recruitment literature, all colleges present themselves as inheritors of the elite system that emerged in the colonial era at Harvard, Princeton, Yale, William and Mary, and other colleges built on the British model. According to Alexander Astin, one of the nation's leading scholars of higher education, the hallmarks of this system were:

- *Educating the undergraduate*

- *Permitting and encouraging close student-student and student-faculty contact*

- *Generating a strong sense of community through history and tradition*

Over the next 250 years, the number and variety of colleges grew and multiplied, producing the various categories of colleges described in Chapter 2: research universities, liberal arts colleges, comprehensive universities, and community colleges. A growing number of for-profit and Internet-based "virtual universities" are emerging, too. The remarkable fact is that most of these institutions—no matter their size or the diversity of their missions—still, according to Astin, "claim to be engaged in the same enterprise; the liberal education of the undergraduate student." In other words, even as higher education grows and diversifies, it still values the ideals of the small, personalized, and student-centered institution.

> *Even as higher education grows and diversifies, it still values the ideals of the small, personalized, and student-centered institution.*

But behind the scenes, the values of an elite system now collide with the realities of a mass system. This disconnect is felt in promotional literature and the happy talk of many campus tours. Colleges and universities walk on a linguistic ledge, portraying themselves as both "large and diverse" as well as "personal and friendly."

Prospective students are usually told that undergraduate learning is the institution's number one priority or that research completed by faculty somehow enhances the quality of undergraduate teaching. In actuality, however, the relationship is sometimes more contentious and real priorities emerge when budget decisions are made. The desire to do well by their undergraduates is usually sincere. Yet as Astin observes in his influential study, *What Matters in College?* "There is a widespread (but seldom publicly stated) belief among university administrators that some of the funds allocated for undergraduate education must be siphoned off to support graduate education and research."

The conflicting values and expectations are also felt in the attitudes of faculty. The rapid expansion and diversification of the undergraduate student body can produce an undercurrent of resentment among some faculty who also cling to the ideals of an elite system. Some lament the arrival of students who appear to be increasingly apathetic, anti-intellectual, and materialistic. Privately, faculty ask, who are these students? They all clamor to get in, but once here they never go to the library, yet they feel entitled to an easy "A."

Conventional wisdom inside the higher education community states that only a small percentage of students—one

> *"The hope is that students will move away from their emphasis on materialism and rather come to see the life of the mind and spirit as being the really crucial aspects of human life."*

quarter, perhaps; one third, at most—arrive at college eager to feast from the full menu of intellectual offerings. The rest move through with less ambition. Newspapers and magazines are filled with stories lamenting the perceived decline in intellectualism among today's students. "Deep Thinkers Missing in Action," summarized a recent headline in the *Christian Science Monitor*. "American higher education has long had a dynamic tension between intellectualism and more practical education," it reported. But the sense among many educators is that the pendulum may be swinging toward a new anti-intellectual approach.

Valparaiso University President Alan Harre acknowledges the conflict in values and expectations. "A typical faculty member is living the life of the mind, the life of the spirit, and the life of aesthetics. He or she got into teaching simply because of his or her love affair with a specific discipline. What these faculty members want from students is a conversion experience. The hope is that students will move away from their emphasis on materialism and come to see the life of the mind and spirit as being the really crucial aspects of human life."

But he readily acknowledges that the vast majority of students will never get there.

It is important to put this criticism into perspective. Complaints about American anti-intellectualism are nothing new. Professors have complained about apathetic students for centuries. To some degree, teachers and students have always lived in different worlds. Even the vast amount of criticism

> *The greatest danger to higher education in the modern era is not materialism and apathy among students, but the failure of colleges and universities to respond to the expanding role of higher education.*

of today's students for their preoccupation with materialism and "careerism" is not new. There never was a "golden age" of higher education when all students and teachers shared a common passion for scholarly pursuits.

However, the greatest danger to higher education in the modern era is not materialism and apathy among students, but the failure of colleges and universities to respond to the expanding role of higher education. Rather than simply resenting student apathy or pandering to it with a narrow and strictly vocational curriculum, the challenge is to offer a curriculum that is intellectually rich and relevant.

Lowering Expectations

Rankings both reflect and reinforce the confusion about higher education. The whole ranking industry emerged at a time when more Americans were going to college and wanted to make the most of their time and money. Yet, ironically, rankings are among the forces that promote

> *Rankings focus attention on a small number of colleges, which limits choices for students and increases stress for applicants determined to get into the "best" schools.*

the most outdated and fossilized understanding of what the college experience is all about. Students and educators alike are encouraged to focus on the symbolic remnants of an elite system—selectivity, reputation, and financial resources. These indicators are viewed as expressions of "quality." However, they tend to reflect and reinforce a much older preoccupation with prestige.

Rankings focus attention on a small number of colleges, which limits choices for students and increases stress for applicants determined to get into the "best" schools. In addition, it encourages a superficial understanding of higher education's benefits. When reputation is the benchmark of quality, the public is encouraged to believe that the institution's name is more important than the educational experience. There is strong evidence that graduation from a highly selective institution does not guarantee a significant economic advantage, but the perception that graduates of brand-name institutions have a head start on prosperity and happiness is firmly entrenched.

Worse still, the harmful influence of rankings reaches far beyond those students and families who limit their choices to top-ranked schools. Rankings also shape the priorities of colleges and university presidents. Administrators understand the weaknesses of rankings, but the allure of being "number one" is irresistible and many presidents will do whatever it takes to climb the rankings ladder. Talking about a broad range of regional state universities, the *Chronicle of Higher Education* recently reported that "every one of them aspires to make it into the top 50, top 20, or top 10 in any number of national rankings."

How do universities improve their reputations? It is usually not by focusing on undergraduate education. Instead, many attempt to buy their prestige. The usual strategy is to hire more top research faculty (often by stealing them away from other universities), recruit more top students (often by using scholarships as financial incentives), and put more money into public relations. "Slick advertising campaigns portray the institutions as being on the cusp of greatness," was how the *Chronicle* summarized the approach. In other words, the focus is on the promotion of research and image—neither of which has much to do with the quality of learning or careful consideration of a twenty-first century curriculum.

These smoke and mirror tactics potentially increase the American public's cynicism and even weaken the institution.

"For all its efforts to improve its rankings, a university may not improve conditions for itself or its community," reported the *Chronicle*. "Pumping money into marquee programs could drain money away from other departments, leaving 'steeples of excellence' surrounded by 'tenements of mediocrity.'"

In this way, the holy grail of a top-tier ranking may actually discourage the kind of innovation and reform that is most needed in higher education. In the end, strategies to improve a university's standing probably do not work.

Irwin Q. Feller, a professor of economics at the Pennsylvania State University who has studied the impact of rankings, says it is very difficult for a university to deliberately improve its standing. "You find a lot of churning—momentary, isolated gains—but the institution really doesn't change much," he says.

Rankings don't work in the best interest of students, nor do they work in the best interest of higher education.

Rankings don't work in the best interest of students, nor do they work in the best interest of higher education. Yet they have gained power because both educators and students lack clear alternatives. There are, however, some emerging attempts to compare college quality in new and more meaningful ways. Frustrated by the abuse and limitations of reputational rankings, educators and policymakers are moving beyond criticism and developing new ways to compare institutions. One of the most promising efforts is the National Survey of Student Engagement (NSSE).

Most Americans have not heard of the NSSE, but soon will. The national survey is an attempt to do what rankings do not—actually measure the degree to which individual colleges and universities create a climate conducive to student learning. The focus is on student engagement—the amount of time and energy actually spent on activities that promote learning. Simply being on campus or sitting in a lecture hall does not prove that learning is taking place. More meaningful evidence of engagement is found when students actively work with faculty and with other students, writing papers and conducting research, reading books, taking part in campus activities, among other benchmarks.

"The engagement premise is deceptively simple, even self-evident," says George Kuh, professor of higher education at Indiana University Bloomington and director of the NSSE project. "The more students study a subject, the more they learn about it. Likewise, the more students practice and get feedback on their writing, analyzing, or problem solving, the more adept they become. The very act of engagement also adds to the list of skills and dispositions that is essential to living a productive, satisfying life after college."

Unlike most rankings, the NSSE is a survey developed by the higher education community and answered by students. Students who participate in the survey are asked a variety of specific questions about how they spend their time and how they are asked to learn. Questions include:

- *How frequently do you participate in class discussions?*

- *How frequently do you study in small groups?*

- *How many books did you read on your own?*

- *How many hours a week do you spend studying?*

Collectively, answers to these and other questions help paint a portrait of student life and intellectual engagement in the nearly 1,000 colleges and universities that participate.

The weakness of the project is that not all institutions choose to participate, and participating colleges and universities reserve the right to withhold certain data. On the other hand, when a college or university feels that it has performed well, you can be sure it will promote the results in college literature.

Overall, the survey has yielded some interesting insights into college life. For example, aggregate results reported from the 2002 survey demonstrated that concerns about disengaged college students are real. While there is much discussion about the value of student participation in faculty research, only 25 percent of seniors reported that they worked on a research paper with a faculty member outside of regular course or program requirements. At the same time, 69 percent of freshmen and 58 percent of seniors also said they never participated in a community-based project as part of a regular course. In addition, while most faculty members believe students need to study at least 25 hours per week, only 14 percent of full-time students met this minimum course requirement. More alarming, 41 percent of students said they spent 10 hours or less hitting the books.

There are bright spots, of course. Many students now take part in service learning programs and an impressive 71 percent said they partici-pated in an internship program or other field experience. Most students also said their campuses are support-ive and welcoming.

> *It is fairly clear that when stu-dent engagement becomes a cri-terion of quality, the most selective schools do not have a guaranteed advantage.*

Overall, students who completed the NSSE said they were less engaged than they hoped to be and less academically chal-lenged than they thought they would be. "What first year stu-dents say they expect to do in college typically exceeds what they actually do. They expect to read more and take part in more cultural activities than they do," says Kuh.

Who, then, are the winners in the NSSE? Because scores of participating schools are not reported for individual insti-tutions, it is not possible to compare findings from the NSSE against reputational surveys, such as that found in *U.S. News & World Report*. However, it is fairly clear that when student engagement becomes a criterion of quality, the most selective schools do not have a guaranteed advantage. Kuh reports that one state's flagship university scored lower than its less presti-gious sister urban university. This finding challenged the long-standing pecking order within that state by contradicting the equally long-standing perception of the relative quality of the institutions within the system.

While liberal arts colleges performed well overall, findings confirm that it is dangerous and unfair to label one type of institution better than another. "While smaller schools generally are more academically challenging, it's also clear that some large universities exceed many smaller colleges on this benchmark," Kuh reports. Many of these institutions represent regional institutions; many do not make it to the top of the *U.S. News* rankings. It appears that engaged colleges exist in all institutional categories and at different levels of selectivity.

Real Quality

Rankings not only guide students, they shape institutions. When reputation and selectivity matter, colleges and universities look for ways to perform well against those benchmarks, but when student learning is the gold standard for excellence, institutions are persuaded to focus

> *While rankings force colleges and universities to play with numbers and push public relations, the NSSE encourages more meaningful reform within institutions.*

more directly on those things that are more likely to improve learning. In this way, the NSSE is not simply another way to compare colleges. Rather, it is "an attempt to shift the nature of the public conversation about collegiate quality," argues Kuh. While rankings force colleges and universities to play with numbers and push public relations, the NSSE encourages more meaningful reform within institutions.

The NSSE is far from perfect, as even its proponents agree. One of the greatest difficulties faced by those who measure the outcomes of education is separating what an institution provided students after they enrolled versus what the students brought with them into the institution. In other words, is the survey identifying institutions that successfully promote engagement or merely colleges that enroll engaged students? This is among those complicated chicken and egg questions that make educational research so messy.

Knowing what higher education should provide empowers students and parents and makes colleges and universities more accountable.

In the end, the value of the NSSE is not that it has perfected the measurement of college quality and can therefore replace reputational rankings, but that it can be part of the renewal of American higher education. This renewal will not take place simply because more meaningful measurements of quality are invented; rather, it will happen when Americans expect more from their colleges and universities. Knowing what higher education should provide empowers students and parents and makes colleges and universities more accountable.

If it is true that higher education is now an essential good—something that all Americans should experience—then colleges and universities need to grow and change in new and radical ways. It must make room for the nearly one third of high school graduates who currently do not enroll; it must find ways to retain more of the 60 percent of students who drop out; and it must do more to make the whole college experience meaningful, even for those who are only focused on earning a credential.

In a very real way, it is up to students and parents to understand the richness of higher education and demand more from the nation's colleges and universities. This means looking for institutions that exemplify the best of what American higher education has to offer. The NSSE is a useful tool or, at least, it *could* be if more institutions would share their data. But Americans need not be prisoners of any survey. Colleges and universities are not mysterious black boxes and it is not that difficult to identify colleges that are genuinely committed to making undergraduate education a rich and meaningful experience.

By focusing on the criteria of quality described in previous chapters, all students can become scholars of higher education and experts on a range of institutions. When students and parents take more control over the college selection process, they can focus more on what matters in higher education and the many subtle factors that define true quality and make college a good fit. When the question becomes "What is the right college for me?" rather than "What is the best college?" we can imagine a time when rankings do not play a role in the college selection process. We can imagine the end of rankings.

epilogue

Every book begins long before the first page is written. This one began on a September morning in 1934 when my father, Ernest Boyer, started first grade.

Growing up in Dayton, Ohio during the Depression, my father remembered how his parents struggled to put food on the table. Survival was a collective effort and even as a young boy he was expected to earn money. He sold trinkets door-to-door and helped his mother and father run a small mail-order business. Their world was narrow and, as part of a tight-knit religious community, had clear boundaries. Work and church defined much of his early life.

But when he turned six, my father slowly became aware of a larger world. He remembered, even years later, his first day of school—the wooden desks, polished hardwood floors, the American flag, and portraits of Presidents Washington and Jefferson. He especially remembered his teacher, Miss Rice, and the first words she said to her class. Standing before her anxious students she announced, "Class, today we learn to read." My father was awed. Of course he believed her. And he did begin to learn.

Education Shapes Lives

What happened over the next twenty years was a story of opportunity shared by many of his generation. My father advanced through school. Not all teachers were as inspired and kind as Miss Rice, but there were moments of encouragement that he remembered for the rest of his life. "Ernest," one high school teacher said, "you're doing well in history. You keep this up and you just might be a student." And he was. While *his* father ended his formal education after high school, my father went directly to college and—breaking precedent yet again—continued on to graduate school. He was the first in his family to earn a Ph.D. This was in 1958.

I think of my father often as I write and talk about the role of education in America because he so clearly symbolized the power education has to change lives. School and college exposed him to new ideas, new people, and new experiences. While he did not renounce his past, he was on a purposeful path of discovery that took him beyond the confines of his childhood home.

Education took him to places he certainly could not have even imagined as a boy. He remained in higher education as a professor and administrator. By 1970 he was head of the nation's largest university system, the State University of New York. By his death in 1995, he had also served as Commissioner of Education for President Carter and spent sixteen years as president of the Carnegie Foundation for the Advancement of Teaching. He authored several highly influential books and reports on elementary, secondary, and higher education. He was, by many accounts, the most influential educator of his era.

Education Shapes Society

During my father's life, America was becoming a mighty world power. But as my father was establishing his career in the post-war years and through the 1960s, there was a great deal of fear and anger—from McCarthyism and the Cuban Missile Crisis to urban riots and Vietnam. Still, deeply imbedded in my father (like much of the nation) was a sense of hope, a feeling that whatever the difficulty, a solution could be found. America could solve poverty, end racism, feed the hungry, and promote justice around the world. It could be a force for peace. We had the resources; all we needed was the will and the right tools.

My father believed that education was one of these tools. Just as it helped him to grow and change as a boy, it could be a force for change for the entire nation. It could do what politics could not. As chancellor of the State University of New York, he initiated a student exchange with the Soviet Union. At the height of the Cold War, a children's theater sponsored by the university traveled to Moscow, performed the *Wizard of Oz*, and sang "Somewhere Over the Rainbow" in Russian. The audience stood, applauded, threw flowers, and cried. "Don't tell me the arts don't matter," my father insisted. The arts can build bridges between peoples, even when they are on the verge of war.

For my father, education was the golden key—not simply to economic opportunity, but also to justice, to compassion, and to empathy. It was an ocean of infinite possibility. It could make the nation better than it already was. "If any single social invention carries with it that potential for the fulfillment of our dreams, it is the university," my father proclaimed in his inaugural speech as chancellor of the State University of New York.

Education was the golden key—not simply to economic opportunity, but also to justice, to compassion, and to empathy.

"I do not for one moment misjudge the urgencies we face," he continued. "They are very real. And yet, ultimately, the issue is not the gravity of the crisis but rather the quality of our response. The strength, the fiber of an institution, as in all of us, is not revealed in tranquil, easy times. Rather, character shines through when adversity looms large and hard choices must be made."

What my father was pursuing went beyond the ability of education to provide jobs, self-esteem, international under-standing, or any other narrowly defined objective. Success of higher education could not be measured solely in salaries or through a nation's gross national product. Instead, my father believed schools and colleges had a broader mandate to support the search for meaning.

Education Matters

One of the most important role models in my father's life was his grandfather, William Boyer. When William was 96 (he would live to be 100), my father asked him about his schooling. "Well," he told my father, "I went to school for about six years, but only in the winter when I wasn't needed on the farm." Yet he was committed to making a difference. When he was 40, William left a factory job and moved his family to the slums of Dayton where he spent the next 40 years running a city mission, providing food and services for the poor—although he was about as poor as the people he helped. My father never forgot his example. "He taught me, as I observed his life, that to be truly human one must serve."

This is the deepest and most profound task of any individual, and of all societies. It is at the heart of wisdom; it is in a very real way, the purpose of education. But it is a purpose all too easily forgotten in the public debate over education. For more than twenty years, the rhetoric of education reform at all levels has focused on promoting greater academic rigor and making the nation more "competitive" in the global marketplace. Mastering the basics, passing standardized exams, and gaining skills and credentials for work are the benchmarks of success in the academic ladder from kindergarten to college.

It is important to ensure that all children gain mastery of fundamental skills. A college degree must also be useful in the marketplace. But to focus on these things alone does not measure the full purpose and value of education. Rigor and competition become ends in themselves, a race with an ever-receding finish line. We tell children and young adults they must learn more, learn harder, and learn faster—but to what end? Something is missing.

There is a strong undercurrent of dissatisfaction among many educators today. The frustration is sometimes directed toward students who do not seem sufficiently grateful to their teachers or who lack a commitment to academics. But the real issues run deeper. Public school teachers and university faculty both want to know that their work and the work of their institution *matters*. They want to know that they are doing more than just awarding credits and moving students through a higher education assembly line. They want to believe that they are touching individual lives, building relationships, and making a difference. They want to know that they are serving students and preparing them for lives of service.

I remember my father describing his first week as Commissioner of Education in the Carter Administration. He was settling into his office in Washington—on the fourth floor of a bland government building called Federal Office Building (or FOB) 6. One of the first requests for a meeting came from the representative of the federal employees union. My father assumed he wanted to talk about salaries and benefits. But when the gentlemen came in, and after pleasantries were exchanged, he asked a very different question. "Mr. Commissioner, can you tell me why we are here?" *Here* meant Washington, in FOB 6, and in the business of looking after the nation's education. What, he wanted to know, were they trying to accomplish?

It would mark great progress if more educators, bureaucrats, elected leaders—and students—would ask this wonderfully provocative question. Great battles are fought over the financing of public education, but rarely are there constructive public debates over the *purpose* of education. Instead, we create tempests in teapots. When education makes headlines, it's usually over small and peripheral issues—substituting Maya Angelou for Shakespeare in a Western Civilization course, for example.

My father believed in education but he was also deeply worried about the future of higher education in America. In a speech to the Academy of Arts and Sciences in 1995, shortly before his death, he said, "Not long ago, it was generally assumed that higher education was an investment in the future of the nation—that the intellect of the nation was something too valuable to lose, and we need to invest in the future through the knowledge industry. But what I find most disturbing," he asserted, "is a growing feeling in this country that higher education is, in fact, part of the problem rather than the solution—going still further, that it's become a private benefit, not a public good. Increasingly, the campus is being viewed as a place where students get credentialed and faculty get tenured, while the overall work of the academy does not seem particularly relevant to the nation's most pressing civic, social, economic, and moral problems."

What was taking place, my father was arguing, was a transformation in the role of higher education. When education becomes *exclusively* a private good and is absolved of any responsibility for serving the public good, it becomes proportionately narrower, and more superficial. It is no longer moored to its deeper purpose of promoting connections and building communities. It becomes a marketable commodity—a product to buy, sell, and value only in economic terms. Education serves the individual aims of individual students, but not the larger objectives of a democratic nation.

Searching for a Curriculum with Coherence

Students and parents feel the impact of this change in some very tangible ways. When education is believed to be a private good—a product that benefits only the student—then students are expected to pay a larger percentage of the cost. Free public higher education is long gone and the percentage of costs borne by students is rising. Long-term prospects for the public subsidy of higher education are dim when neither the public nor the policymakers view higher education as serving a greater social good.

But the deeper purposes of education can be restored, my father believed. What was required was not necessarily more classes, more years of study, or harder exams. Instead, institutions of higher education should be dedicated—or rededicated—to the education of citizens. For much of my father's later career, he investigated and promoted those things that could accomplish these ends.

He believed that at the heart of the renewal of higher education was an integrated curriculum, what he called a "curriculum with coherence"—a strong general education program, the mastery of writing and speaking, and a program of study that showed how all knowledge was connected and "useful."

> *"What we need in the academy are scholar-citizens—people who are committed to building an intellectual community, not just in the classroom but in the coffee shop and committee room as well."*

He often noted Albert Einstein's assertion that religion, art, and the sciences are branches of the same tree. He quoted Barbara McClintock, a Nobel Prize-winning geneticist, who once told him "everything is one."

An integrated curriculum was vital. But to serve students and society at large, more was needed. He viewed colleges and universities as more than classrooms and libraries; they were learning *communities*. He worried about the narrow specialization of the academic departments, a focus on research that relegated teaching to a second-class function. "What we need in the academy are scholar-citizens—people who are committed to building an intellectual community, not just in the classroom but in the coffee shop and committee room as well."

In the end, my father believed education was more than a diploma. It was an opportunity for each individual to grow as a human being. "I know how idealistic it may sound," he said in 1993, "but it is my urgent hope that in the century ahead students in the nation's schools will be judged not by their performance on a single test but by the quality of their lives. It's my hope that students in the classrooms of tomorrow will be encouraged to be creative, not conforming, learning to co-operate rather than compete."

My father was filled with hope for education, and for America. Yet during his lifetime higher education became more specialized, more competitive, more of a commodity and less of a public service. A preoccupation with prestige and credentials is now stronger than ever. Is my father's vision still meaningful in the twenty-first century? Or must we simply allow higher education to change with the times? In other words, are students—and the nation—so different today that we can expect less from higher education?

Becoming a Student

As the product of a later generation, education played a different role in my life. I grew up in a time of prosperity. Opportunities seemed limitless and television was my first teacher. When I was five I recall my mother telling me about a new children's show on PBS. This was 1969 and I became the first generation to watch *Sesame Street*. When my father asked me in mock surprise where I had learned my ABCs, I told him, "My kindergarten teacher thinks she taught me, but I really learned it on *Sesame Street*." Unlike my father, I don't remember my first-grade teacher. What could she teach me? Thanks to Big Bird, I already knew how to read.

School was less of a door into a new world than a well-traveled corridor, an expectation more than a privilege. I took it for granted most of the time, although I had several very good teachers growing up. In my last years of high school, education felt downright constraining. I had an old car and my own hobbies and intellectual interests. What happened between 7:30 a.m. and 2:30 p.m. was, most of the time, a tedious interruption in an otherwise exciting world.

When it came time to go to college, I briefly considered taking a year off. But what would I do? Everyone around me was applying to college and no one offered encouragement for an alternate path. Relenting, I chose a small liberal arts college in the Midwest. It seemed friendly and, if nothing else, I looked forward to living on my own. But while the curriculum was creative and the teachers committed, I still felt uninspired. I liked having long, thoughtful conversations in the coffee shop with my friends, but I fell asleep in astronomy class.

I dropped out, saved money from a newspaper internship, and spent several months traveling through Central America. I wrote a couple of stories that appeared in a mid-sized paper in New Jersey. To some, perhaps, my impulsive decisions may have seemed reckless and irresponsible. But I felt that, at last, something was happening in my life—something meaningful. I was tired of being a kid; I felt ready to make a difference.

When I returned to college the following year, I found an institution that provided the kind of flexibility I needed. I enrolled in Empire State College, an alternative "college without walls" within the State University of New York. Empire State didn't have traditional campuses or classes. Instead, students worked one-on-one with faculty "mentors." Together, the student and mentor developed " learning contracts"— objectives that students would fulfill through independent study, work, internships, and by taking classes at other institutions.

Interested in Latin American politics and journalism, I returned to Central America, taught at an American school in Costa Rica, studied Spanish at a language institute, wrote articles for newspapers—and earned credit for each experience.

My mentor back in the U.S. was Dr. Ken Abrams. He, like Miss Rice, deserves to be mentioned by name because he was the one who made me feel like education mattered. Like my father's high school history teacher, he told me I was a *student.* Every few months, I would travel to New York City and meet with Ken in his cluttered office. There we would discuss my experiences, my progress, and my hopes for the future. I would leave his office an hour or two later feeling that he took me seriously—as a scholar, and as a person. College wasn't an institution anymore. It was a relationship, and that made all the difference.

I completed my degree and continued my education through more traditional graduate programs. Since then, I have also remained a part of education as both a writer and teacher. In one capacity or another, I have taught or studied in nearly every type

> *College wasn't an institution anymore. It was a relationship, and that made all the difference.*

of college available in America—liberal arts college, research university, community college, distance learning center. Large, small, prestigious, obscure: the diversity of American higher education has become my world, as well.

Hope for the Twenty-first Century

This book is, in the end, a blend of experiences. From my father comes a faith in the power of education to serve society and, especially, a specific understanding of what excellence means in undergraduate education. The key indicators of college quality promoted in this book—freshman-year programs, internships, a strong campus community, among others—are drawn directly from his own research and a book he and I coauthored in 1996 called the *Smart Parents Guide to College*. I am pleased to see that a growing number of colleges and educational institutions are embracing these specific programs and their objectives.

From my own experience and research, however, comes a strong belief that today's students must be wise and cautious consumers in what has become a competitive and hyped education marketplace. In a market-driven environment, I am convinced that students must

> *By looking for institutions committed to teaching, service, and the practical liberal arts, students can promote richer and more meaningful approaches to learning.*

know what matters in higher education and know how to evaluate their options. Students, more than college administrators, will determine the future of undergraduate education in America. For better or worse, higher education will become what they and the public demand. By looking for institutions committed to teaching, service, and the practical liberal arts, students can promote richer and more meaningful approaches to learning.

From both my father and myself comes a passionate belief that colleges and universities must become more diverse and more flexible. America needs to expand its understanding of education if it is to fulfill its mandate to serve all members of society. Earlier in this book, I talked about the rich diversity of American higher education. In many ways, this is true. But I also worry that most colleges and universities are more alike than different. How they teach, what they teach, and how they organize the curriculum differs only in small ways across the spectrum of institutions. The patterns of academic life for students at an Ivy League university in New England and a rural community college in North Dakota are almost identical—seat time in a classroom, three credits a class, and twelve or fifteen credits a semester. Stay long enough and you get a diploma.

My greatest hope is that education will become less homogenous in the twenty-first century. If we are heading toward an era of true lifelong learning then we need approaches to education that seamlessly blend the college experience with what undergraduates like to call "real life." We need to provide even traditional students with opportunities to leave the classroom and serve their communities. We need to expand the definition of scholarship to include both teaching and public service. We need institutions that touch lives beyond the campus community. Let's go even further. If we're now all students, then why not establish opportunities for earning and "banking" of credit for knowledge gained through work, travel, and self-study throughout a lifetime? And why not promote mid-life sabbaticals, where any adult (not just tenured professors) can spend up to a year engaged in research or volunteer service?

Let's break down walls—physical and conceptual—between the scholarship of academe and the scholarship of experience.

Critics of higher education often say Americans expect too much from their schools and colleges. Not surprisingly, colleges and universities are not equal to the challenge. "The history of American education is the triumph of hope over experience," education writers Fred and Grace Hechinger acknowledged in *Growing Up in America*. "Excessive expectations have produced excessive disenchantment. Angry critics reflect the gap between schools' promises and their performance." Indeed, the long history of education advocacy has also produced a long history of criticism. If education can build a stronger society, then why is America still so imperfect?

While more American's are going to college, the gap between rich and poor has widened in recent years. Poverty and hunger are still with us, as is ignorance in many and various forms. Education is believed to be a function of civilized societies. But despite mass education, there seems to be no discernable increase in civility. The Puritans arrived in a new world expecting to establish a "city on a hill." They started the nation's first college in a wilderness and began educating a small handful of scholars. Today we have more colleges than any other nation and one of the world's most highly educated populations. Yet can we say that we are now a "city on a hill"?

Thinking about the gap between the rhetoric and reality of higher education is important. But it is also true that schools and colleges are the only public institutions with a mandate to question and to argue for change. Where else do we go in society when we want to not simply celebrate who we are as a nation, but think about what we might become? What other public institution embraces the idea that people are more than workers and consumers? If this understanding is lost—either out of apathy or cynicism—then I worry that we will be diminished as citizens and as a nation.

My father often recalled part of a poem by Vachel Lindsey:

> *It is the world's one crime*
> *its babes grow dull,*
> *....*
> *Not that they sow,*
> *but that they seldom reap,*
> *Not that they serve,*
> *but have no gods to serve,*
> *Not that they die*
> *but that they die like sheep.*

In a 1993 speech my father concluded: "The tragedy is not death. The tragedy is to die with commitments undefined, conviction undeclared, and service unfulfilled. And with all the controversy that surrounds it, a school must be a place where values are examined, not by dictating answers, but by making honorable the quest."

appendix a

Resources

Educators spend a great deal of time thinking and writing about their profession. In professional journals and conferences, many higher education leaders are asking:

- *What should students learn?*
- *What are the best ways to teach?*
- *How do we know that students are learning and are prepared for the future?*

However, most of this scholarship is shared only with other educators. When educators talk to the public, the conversation is far more superficial and self-serving. It often boils down to the simple statement: "You should go to college (preferably our college) because it's good for you." This may help explain why rankings and "insider guides" dominate the market. Despite their flaws, they are the only publications that *attempt* to get beyond the rhetoric of public relations and hold institutions accountable.

Fortunately, there are some higher education associations that are conducting research and publishing reports that are readable and provide useful information for students and parents, including:

American Association of Collegiate Registrars and Admissions Officers (AACRAO)

http://www.aacrao.org/

The mission of the American Association of Collegiate Registrars and Admissions Officers is to provide professional development, guidelines, and voluntary standards to be used by higher education officials regarding the best practices in records management, admissions, enrollment management, administrative information technology, and student services. It also provides a forum for discussion regarding policy initiation and development, interpretation and implementation at the institutional level and in the global educational community.

Association of American Colleges and Universities (AAC&U)

http://www.aacu-edu.org/index.cfm

The AAC&U is the leading national association concerned with the quality, vitality, and public standing of undergraduate liberal education. Today, it represents the entire spectrum of American colleges and universities: large and small, public and private, two-year and four-year.

In recent years, the AAC&U has challenged the widespread assumption that liberal education can be achieved only in selected disciplines, or in small colleges. Current work, however, focuses on the overall aims of liberal learn-

ing and on ways to achieve these aims across the entire educational experience, for all students and in every kind of
college and university.

American Association of Community Colleges (AACC)

http://www.aacc.nche.edu/

The American Association of Community Colleges has been
a national voice for two-year associate degree granting institutions since 1920. Located in the National Center for
Higher Education in Washington, D.C., the AACC works
with other higher education associations, the federal government, Congress, and other national associations that represent the public and private sectors to promote the goals
of community colleges and higher education.

The American Association for Higher Education (AAHE)

http://www.aahe.org/about.htm

The AAHE is the membership organization that serves its
members, other individuals, communities, and institutions
in the higher education community by building their capacity as learners and leaders and increasing their effective-
ness in a complex, interconnected world.

To pursue these aims, the AAHE:

- *Envisions and articulates agendas for change*

- *Contributes to systemic improvement in higher education*

- *Convenes forums for constructive conversations about difficult issues*

- *Advocates learning practices that help individuals and institutions benefit from diversity*

- *Documents and promotes multiple forms of scholarship*

- *Enables institutions to achieve their evolving missions*

- *Collaborates with individuals and organizations engaged in complementary work*

- *Disseminates the body of knowledge on teaching and learning*

American Association of State Colleges and Universities (AASCU)

http://www.aascu.org/

The American Association of State Colleges and Universities advocates for the improvement of public higher education. The AASCU represents more than 430 public colleges, universities, and systems of public higher education.

American Council on Education (ACE)

http://www.acenet.edu/

The American Council on Education, founded in 1918, is the nation's coordinating higher education association. The ACE is dedicated to the belief that equal educational opportunity and a strong higher education system are essential cornerstones of a democratic society. Its approximately 1,800 members include accredited, degree-granting colleges and universities from all sectors of higher education and other education and education-related organizations.

Association for the Study of Higher Education (ASHE)

http://www.ashe.ws

The Association for the Study of Higher Education is a scholarly society with about 1,400 members dedicated to higher education as a field of study. The Association promotes collaboration among its members and others engaged in the study of higher education through research, conferences, and publications, including its highly regarded journal, *The Review of Higher Education*. The ASHE values rigorous scholarly approaches to the study of higher education and practical applications of systemic inquiry. It is committed to diversity in its programs and membership, and has enjoyed extraordinary success in involving graduate students in Association activities.

Campus Compact
http://www.compact.org/

Campus Compact is a national coalition of more than 900 college and university presidents committed to the civic purposes of higher education. To support this civic mission, Campus Compact promotes community service that develops students' citizenship skills and values, encourages partnerships between campuses and communities, and assists faculty who seek to integrate public and community engagement into their teaching and research.

The Carnegie Foundation for the Advancement of Teaching
http://www.carnegiefoundation.org/index.htm

The Carnegie Foundation for the Advancement of Teaching is an independent policy and research center whose charge is "to do and perform all things necessary to encourage, uphold, and dignify the profession of the teacher and the cause of higher education."

Its mission is to address the hardest problems faced in teaching in public schools, colleges and universities—that is, how to succeed in the classroom, how best to achieve lasting student learning, and how to assess the impact of teaching on students.

Carnegie Scholars Program

http://www.carnegiefoundation.org/CASTL/highered/scholars_program.htm

The Carnegie Scholars Program brings together outstanding faculty committed to investigating and documenting significant issues in teaching and learning. The program is not an award for teaching excellence, nor is it a teaching-improvement workshop. Its purpose is to create a community of scholars, diverse in all the ways that matter in teaching and learning, whose work will advance the profession of teaching and deepen student learning.

Council of Independent Colleges (CIC)

http://www.cic.edu/

Founded in 1956 and based in Washington, D.C., the Council of Independent Colleges is an association of nearly 500 independent, liberal arts colleges and universities that work together to support college leadership, advance institutional excellence, and enhance private higher education's contributions to society.

Working with college presidents, academic vice presidents, other administrators, and faculty, CIC provides services that help its member institutions enhance educational programs, improve their administrative and financial performance, and increase their institutional visibility.

DiversityWeb

http://www.diversityweb.org/

DiversityWeb is a project of the AAC&U's Office of Diversity, Equity, and Global Initiatives (ODEGI). Central to the office's mission is the belief that diversity and global knowledge are essential elements of any effort to foster civic engagement among today's college students. To support those goals, the office helps colleges and universities establish diversity as a comprehensive institutional commitment and educational priority.

Providing national leadership, ODEGI supports colleges and universities in their efforts to create settings that foster students' understanding of the intersection between domestic and global issues and their sense of responsibility as local and global citizens. The AAC&U works with campuses to cultivate productive public dialogues and community partnership to enhance democratic values and practices in our diverse but still unequal American society.

Educational Quality Accrediting Commission (EQAC)

http://www.eqac.org/

The EQAC is an international and independent body, which examines and evaluates higher education institutions from every country to promote sound education and good business practices. The EQAC is today's international point of reference for people, companies, and colleges and universities concerned about the quality of higher education.

Institute for Higher Education Policy

http://www.ihep.com/

The mission of the Institute for Higher Education Policy is to foster access and success in postsecondary education through public policy research and other activities that inform and influence the policymaking process

Founded in 1993, the Institute informs the policymaking process in collaboration with U.S. state, federal, and institutional level partners, and internationally in countries such as South Africa, Mozambique, and Russia.

The Institute draws on the combined expertise of its senior associates and researchers, whose ranks include some of the leading policy analysts in higher education.

Institute on College Student Values
http://www.collegevalues.org/institute.cfm

The Institute on College Student Values is an annual conference for student affairs professionals, educators, campus ministers, and other individuals interested in character development in college students. First held in 1991, the Institute is concerned with five broad areas of interest:

- *Trends in student values*
- *Ethical issues in college life*
- *Character building educational models and strategies*
- *Moral development research*
- *Civic education*

The Institute provides an opportunity to learn about the most current issues, research, and educational activities pertaining to character education in college. In addition, the Institute is designed to be a "think tank" for individuals who have particular interests in exploring more effective ways to promote civic education and the ethical development of college students.

National Academy for Academic Leadership
http://www.thenationalacademy.org

The National Academy for Academic Leadership educates academic decision makers to be leaders for sustained, integrated institutional change that significantly improves student learning. Its curriculum is based on research and best practices. Its programs are designed both for institutional teams working on campus projects and for individuals—presidents, board members, vice presidents, deans, chairs, and key faculty members—with role-specific responsibilities and concerns. The National Academy recognizes the considerable variation among institutions in their readiness for change and their resources for leadership development, and so programs are geared to the unique institutional contexts and specific needs of participants.

National Association of Independent Colleges and Universities (NAICU)
http://www.naicu.edu/

The National Association of Independent Colleges and Universities serves as the unified national voice of independent higher education. Since 1976, the Association has represented private colleges and universities on policy issues with the federal government, such as those affecting student aid, taxation, and government regulation. Today, through new communication technologies, an improved governance structure, and increased member participation, the NAICU has become an even more effective and respected participant in the political process.

National Center for Public Policy and Higher Education

http://www.highereducation.org/

As an independent, nonprofit, nonpartisan organization, the National Center promotes public policies that enhance Americans' opportunities to pursue and achieve high-quality education and training beyond high school. The National Center recently completed Measuring Up 2000, a state-by-state report card for higher education.

National Society for Experiential Education (NSEE)

http://www.nsee.org/

The NSEE supports the use of learning through experience for intellectual development, cross-cultural and global awareness, civic and social responsibility, ethical development, career exploration, and personal growth.

The National Survey of Student Engagement (NSSE)

http://www.indiana.edu/~nsse/

The NSSE attempts to measure the degree to which students actively participate in the learning process. Students answer questions about how they spend their time out of class, how frequently they interact with faculty, and how many hours they spend studying, among other questions that explore levels of student "engagement."

The NSSE discourages the use of the survey for any kind of ranking and does not publicly report results of individual institutions. It is up to prospective students to ask participating institutions if survey results are available to the public.

Reinventing Undergraduate Education: A Blueprint for America's Research Universities

http://naples.cc.sunysb.edu/Pres/boyer.nsf/

This 1998 report released through Stony Brook University in New York examines the status of undergraduate education at research universities and describes how these institutions can strengthen student learning through the promotion of research-based learning, freshman seminars, and strong writing requirements, among other strategies. It highlights the special opportunities and challenges facing research universities working to make their institutions more responsive to the needs of undergraduate students.

Western Interstate Commission for Higher Education (WICHE)

http://www.wiche.edu/About/index.htm

The Western Interstate Commission for Higher Education is a regional organization created by the Western Regional Education Compact, adopted in the 1950s by Western states. WICHE is an interstate compact created by formal legislative action of the states and the U.S. Congress. WICHE was created to facilitate resource sharing among the higher education systems of the West. It has implemented a number of regional activities to accomplish its objectives.

appendix b

Questions to Determine Quality

Summarized here are the fifteen key questions to ask when investigating a college or university. Collectively, they help identify institutions that make a real commitment to serving the needs of undergraduate students. See chapter 4 for more information about these questions and the five indicators of college quality.

A Commitment to General Education

General education is an integral part of a quality undergraduate education. More than a random collection of introductory courses that students try to "get out of the way," a carefully crafted sequence of general education courses builds real skills in writing, researching, and critical thinking. It also broadens and deepens the knowledge and skills taught within each student's major field of study.

Although there is no one "right" way to teach general education, prospective students should look for evidence that the colleges and universities they are considering make it a real priority. This means looking for institutions that create courses specifically for the general education program, and integrate general education courses throughout all four or more years of learning.

1. Does the college or university offer freshman-year seminars?

- *Do all or most freshmen enroll in one or more freshman-year seminars?*

- *Are freshman-year seminars optional or required?*

- *Are these courses taught by full-time faculty?*

2. Does general education extend from the freshman year to the senior year?

- *Does the college or university offer a core curriculum (a sequence of required courses) or a carefully developed set of distribution requirements? If distribution requirements are used, students should pick from a limited list of classes that, preferably, have been created just for the general education program.*

- *How many general education courses are listed in the institution's course catalog?*

- *Do the courses appear to be connected to each other? Avoid colleges or universities that offer a long list of optional classes that are disconnected from each other and from the rest of the curriculum.*

A Commitment to Writing, Speaking, and Critical-Thinking Skills

Communication skills are vital for success in college, and in all careers. Whether taught formally through an English composition class, or integrated into a freshman seminar, written and oral communication should be a priority during the first year of study. When investigating institutions, make sure writing skills are formally taught through these or similar courses. Equally important, writing should be an integral part of many—preferably most—classes taken during all four or more years of study.

3. Are English language skills formally taught during the freshman year?

- *Are one or more English composition courses required?*

- *Are communication skills formally developed in a freshman seminar or similar course?*

4. Are writing and speaking required in every subject during all years of study?

- *Are students required to complete at least two writing-intensive courses during their years of study?*

- *Are writing-intensive classes a part of every major?*

5. Is writing emphasized in every class?

- *Do all teachers value the importance of writing?*

A Commitment to Active Learning

Active learning is found on campuses where all undergraduate students—from the freshman to the senior year—are encouraged to do more than take notes and pass tests. Students at these institutions work closely with faculty, take part in class discussions, complete team projects with fellow students, and participate in real research with faculty. All this helps to create a richer, more meaningful education.

6. Do teachers know their students?

- *What is the average undergraduate class size?*

- *What are the largest and smallest classes taught?*

- *How big is the largest required general education class?*

- *If large lecture classes are offered, are they accompanied by small discussion sections?*

7. Do students participate in class?

- *Are first-year and introductory classes taught as seminars where students participate in classroom discussions?*

- *Do students regularly work in small groups?*

- *Are students encouraged to collaborate on assignments and special projects?*

8. Do students spend time with faculty outside the classroom?

- *Are formal programs offered that encourage student and faculty interaction outside the classroom?*

9. Do most students participate in faculty research?

- *What is the percentage of students that assist faculty members with research?*

- *Are all students expected to complete their own original research—such as a senior thesis—before graduation?*

Opportunities to Extend Learning Beyond the Classroom

A quality college or university recognizes that learning takes place both inside and outside the classroom. It encourages, and possibly even requires, students to enrich their academic experiences through internships, service learning, and international study. For many students, these experiences become the most memorable and meaningful part of their education and nurture the skills and confidence needed in the workforce.

10. Do most students learn beyond the classroom?

- *What percentage of students take part in internships and overseas travel?*

- *Do students earn academic credit for internships and travel experiences?*

- *How are students guided and advised as they complete off-campus studies?*

11. Is service learning part of the curriculum?

- *What percentage of students participate in service-learning programs?*

- *Is academic credit offered for service learning?*

A Diverse, Intellectually Active, and Respectful Community

Colleges and universities are more than classrooms; they are communities. How students spend their time out of class is just as important as what they study in class. At quality colleges and universities, students feel safe, are treated with respect, and have ample opportunities to participate in a rich menu of extracurricular programs.

12. Is the college or university a safe community?

- *Does the college or university make its crime statistics available to prospective students?*

- *Does the college or university help to ensure safety through a campus police force, escort services, adequate lighting, and other strategies?*

- *Do current students feel safe?*

- *Are current students satisfied with campus security?*

13. Is the college or university a respectful community?

- *Is the college or university's code of conduct respected by students, staff, and faculty?*

14. Is the college or university a creative, intellectually engaged community?

- *Does the college or university host a wide variety of speakers, artists, and performers?*

- *What percentage of students participate in clubs, student government, sports, and other extracurricular activities?*

15. Does the college or university promote diversity?

- *Does the student body reflect the diversity of America?*

- *Are different cultures and values reflected in the curriculum and celebrated across campus?*

- *Is an international perspective emphasized?*

index

A

Active learning, 98–100

     barriers to, 103–04

     commitment to, 107–27

     defined, 126

Admissions

     applicant acceptance rates, 50

     parental involvement, 38–40

American Council on Education, 163, 165

America's Best Colleges, 19, 43

Anderson, Loren, 91, 99

Anti-intellectual criticism, 167–69

Applicant acceptance rates, 50

Assessment of success

     National Survey of Student Engagement (NSSE), 173–79

     senior projects, 154–55

     senior seminars, 152–53

     skills, 164–65

     student outcomes, 154–56

Association of American Colleges and Universities (AAC&U), 91–92, 95, 98

Astin, Alexander, 166–67

B

Bird, Carolyn, 162–63

Bush, Frank, 130

C

U

U. S. News & World Report ranking system

> controversy surrounding, 41–43
>
> measurement methodology, 41–43
>
> value of, 19–21

V

Veblen, Thorstein, 73

Veysey, Laurence, 73

Virtual universities, 166

Vocational education, 33, 77, 81, 84, 169

W

What Matters in College? (Astin), 167

Woodbury, Robert L., 50

Writing skills, 94–97, 100, 103, 107, 112–15, 120–25